The WARREN COURT and the PUBLIC SCHOOLS

An Analysis of Landmark Supreme Court Decisions

H. C. HUDGINS, JR.

THE WARREN COURT
AND THE
PUBLIC SCHOOLS

THE WARREN COURT AND THE PUBLIC SCHOOLS

An Analysis of Landmark Supreme Court Decisions

by

H. C. HUDGINS, JR.

*Associate Professor
Educational Administration
Temple University*

**THE INTERSTATE
PRINTERS & PUBLISHERS, INC.**

Danville, Illinois

1977

ANDOVER-HARVARD THEOLOGICAL LIBRARY
HARVARD DIVINITY SCHOOL

Copyright © 1970
by
THE INTERSTATE
PRINTERS & PUBLISHERS, INC.

All Rights Reserved

Library of Congress
Catalog Card Number: 76-121632

Printed in U.S.A.

Dedicated to

E. C. Bolmeier

—*scholar, teacher, and friend.*

FOREWORD

The decisions of the Warren Court dealing with education have had a very significant impact upon it throughout the entire nation. Much has been written about the individual decisions, but so far as I know this volume represents the first complete coordinated coverage. The author's plan of organization is to analyze each of the cases related to a particular topic and then to coordinate the findings of all the cases on the more specific aspects of the issues involved. This practice seems to bring into focus more sharply the reasoning of the court on these issues. The decisions have all been analyzed very carefully, and every aspect of each decision has been considered. The author's conclusions seem to be entirely correct.

This volume should be very helpful. It will be of interest to and meet the needs of a good many people who are directing and working in our public schools.

Newton Edwards

CONTENTS

FOREWORD vii

I. INTRODUCTION 1
    The Supreme Court 1

II. BACKGROUND 7
    Religion 7
    Segregation 14
    Academic Freedom 19

III. RELIGION 25
    Introduction 25
    The Cases 27
    Free Exercise and Establishment 43
    Religion in Opening Exercises 50
    Standing to Sue 51
    Coercion in Religious Exercises 53
    Voluntary Participation 54
    Rights of the Majority and Minority 55
    Government Neutrality 55
    State Sponsorship and Endorsement 57
    Sectarianism and Secularism 58
    Financing Religious Exercises 59
    Related Religious Activities 61
    Summary 68

IV. SEGREGATION 73
    Introduction 73
    The Cases 76
    Relief 94

  Delay in Compliance 97
  Equal Treatment 99
  Intangible Factors 100
  State Action 102
  Racial Classifications 105
  Overthrow of *Plessy* 106
  Standards of Desegregation 107
  Compulsory Integration of the Races 110
  Summary 112

V. ACADEMIC FREEDOM 119

  Introduction 119
  The Cases Involving Freedom of Association of Teachers 121
  Common Elements of the Cases 137
  The Cases Involving Loyalty Oaths 139
  Common Elements of the Cases 148
  Summary 149

VI. CONCLUDING SUMMARY 155

  Religion 155
  Segregation 157
  Academic Freedom 159

TABLE OF CASES 161

SELECTED BIBLIOGRAPHY 165

INDEX 173

Chapter I

INTRODUCTION

The Supreme Court

Article III of the United States Constitution provides for the federal judiciary system. It creates "one supreme Court" and provides for "such inferior Courts as the Congress may from time to time ordain and establish." The Supreme Court, circuit courts of appeal, and district courts have been created through the article. In addition, there are other courts, such as the Court of Claims, expressly for the purpose of handling specialized problems.

Appointment to the United States Supreme Court is considered to be one of the highest honors an American citizen can receive. The requirements for selection are few. A justice is appointed by the President, subject to confirmation by the Senate. The term of office is for life or, as the Constitution states, "during good Behavior." A justice can be removed only for "Impeachment for, and Conviction of, Treason, Bribery, or other high Crime and Misdemeanors." In the nation's history no justice has ever been found guilty of crime, although Samuel Chase was impeached.

Justices may elect to retire from the Court. With a minimum of fifteen years of service, a justice may retire at age sixty-five with benefit of his full salary for life. Many justices have served many years on the Court. When he retired in 1932, Oliver Wendell Holmes was ninety and had twenty-nine years of service. Eight justices served thirty years or longer—Chief Justice John Marshall, Bushrod Washington, William Johnson, Joseph Story, John McLean, James Moore Wayne, Stephen Field, and John Marshall Harlan, grandfather of the present justice with the same name. Of the justices serving in June 1969, Hugo Black had the longest tenure with thirty-two years on the bench, two more than William O. Douglas. When they took the oath at age thirty-two, Story and Johnson became the youngest to have been appointed to the Court.

The Constitution also describes the Court's jurisdiction according to the nature of the case the Court hears. Original jurisdiction is exercised over disputes "affecting Ambassadors, other public Ministers and

Consuls, and those in which a State shall be Party." Other cases reach the Court on appeal from lower federal courts or the highest tribunals of the states. The appeal may take one of two forms. Most of the decisions are the result of a request for a writ of *certiorari,* meaning that a party to the dispute has disagreed with the court's ruling and requests the Supreme Court to review the case. The other appeal is through a writ of error wherein a party, believing the decision to have been arrived at incorrectly, requests a review by the highest court.

Of the three branches of government provided by the Constitution, the Supreme Court is unique. Unlike members of the Congress and the President, justices are appointed to their positions. A justice's term is for life; the President, four years; Senators, six years; and members of the House of Representatives, two years.

The justices are charged with fulfilling the promise to Americans of "equal justice under law," an inscription which appears over the entrance to the Supreme Court Building. However, once the justices have rendered a decision, there is no recourse of appeal; this again makes the Supreme Court unique. The only remedy for countering a decision is through a Congressional statute or an amendment to the Constitution. Usually, the Supreme Court is the last resort sought by those who claim to have been deprived of some fundamental right.

The subject matter of the cases usually determines whether the Supreme Court will agree to render a decision. In making this decision the justices must exercise some discrimination. It would be impossible for the justices to hear arguments and render decisions on the approximately 3,000 appeals they receive annually. Therefore, the justices review the petitions and accept those cases involving a significant federal or Constitutional question or some allegedly serious wrong. Before the Court can accept an appeal, four of the justices must vote to agree to hear the case. Since each justice is assigned to one of the eleven federal circuits, he helps to screen the petitions for review originating in his circuit. The Clerk of Court of the Supreme Court also assists in an administrative capacity by receiving and processing cases.

To provide further assistance to members of the Court, law clerks are assigned to the justices. These men, representing the country's ablest graduates of law schools, are appointed by the justices. Each justice is assigned two law clerks except the Chief Justice who has three. Bryon R. White, clerk to the late Chief Justice Fred Vinson, is the only clerk to have later been selected as a justice.

The work of the Court is made easier by pages who serve as messengers and run errands. In addition, the justices have secretaries and other staff personnel. The Supreme Court Building is stocked with a

INTRODUCTION

large library, available not only to the justices but also to other persons.

A yearly session of the Court lasts from October until June. Traditionally, the justices convene on the first Monday in October. When arguments are being held, citizens may attend the sessions and watch the proceedings, The Court alternates in holding open arguments on Mondays through Thursdays and in having closed sessions for discussing cases and researching precedents and related opinions.

After the justices have voted on a case, one of them is assigned the task of writing the opinion. In the event that some justices agree with the decision but disagree with the rationale, they may decide to write a concurring opinion. If a justice disagrees with the decision, he may write a dissenting opinion. While concurring and dissenting opinions have no legal standing, they do reflect the thinking of the justices. Moreover, in close decisions, a minority or dissenting opinion may later become the decision of the majority. Strict secrecy is maintained throughout the time the justices are considering a case until the decision is announced.

Formerly, the Court gave its decisions only on Monday. However, in 1965, Chief Justice Earl Warren announced that the Court would deliver opinions on other days as well. The justice writing the opinion reads it from the bench, and copies are instantly available. Provision for this has been made possible by the Court's own printing machine located in the building. Permanent records of the decisions may be studied in *United States Reports.*

When the Court is in session, the justices convene in the Court Room at ten o'clock with traditional practices governing the proceedings. The Marshal uses an Anglo-French cry, "Oyez, Oyez, Oyez," to silence all persons in attendance. The justices come through red velvet draperies to take their seats in chairs custom-made to each justice's specifications. Seating of the justices is in order of seniority with the Chief Justice occupying the middle chair. On his right is the ranking associate justice; on his left, the next ranking associate justice and proceeding thus alternately. This means that the newest justice is seated to the Chief Justice's extreme left.

Tradition further guides the Court's deliberations in sessions not open to the public. In discussing the merits of a case, each justice is given the opportunity to contribute his opinions on the issue. Arguments begin with the Chief Justice and proceed with the associate justices in the order of seniority. When a vote is taken on a case, the most recent appointee casts his vote first, followed in an ascending order according to seniority. After the vote is taken a justice is selected to write the Court's opinion. If the Chief Justice votes with the majority, he makes the assignment; if he does not, the ranking associate justice in the majority appoints the author. The writer then makes a draft, seeks the approval of the justices voting with him, and reworks the manuscript before it becomes official.

For the most part, nine justices have comprised the membership of the Court, although the number has varied within the country's history. Since George Washington appointed the first justices in 1789, there have been ninety-seven persons to serve on the bench. Of that number, fifteen have been Chief Justice.

Within recent years people have been outspoken in their disagreement with some Supreme Court decisions. Attacks have ranged from critical highway bulletin boards to suggestions of impeachment of the justices. The justices have been charged with exceeding their authority, making legislative rather than judicial pronouncements, and stripping the states of their rights. Individual justices have been criticized for their activity both on and off the bench. For the first time in the Court's history, a justice resigned under pressure when it was discovered that Abe Fortas was receiving an annual stipend for serving as counsel to a firm whose principal officer had been sentenced to prison for stock manipulations.

Criticisms of the Court have stemmed in particular from decisions affecting religion and segregation in the public schools.

Since members of the Court remain somewhat detached from the public, they do not answer their critics. Although the justices render their decisions and explain the constitutional bases for arriving at these decisions, they do not defend their action beyond what is stated in the opinion. Therefore, one can best understand what the Supreme Court has said through an examination of the decisions.

This volume is an examination, analysis, and interpretation of public school cases decided by the Supreme Court of the United States from the time Earl Warren took the oath as Chief Justice on October 5, 1953 until his retirement on June 23, 1969.

It is recognized at the outset that such a study could encompass a myriad of tangential problems and issues such as those touching on sociology and theology. However, instead of treating these extraneous but vital questions, the writer limits himself to questions of law. Further, there is no attempt to determine whether the Court ruled wisely or unwisely; rather, the author accepts the decisions themselves as being law. The real justification for this investigation is in helping to clarify what the Court has actually said in its decisions.

The Warren Court has rendered decisions affecting three subject

INTRODUCTION

areas of the schools: religion, segregation, and academic freedom. These subjects are treated in three separate chapters. In addition, a background chapter is included which reviews pertinent decisions of the Supreme Court prior to October 1953.

Chapter II

BACKGROUND

The number of cases decided prior to 1953 by the United States Supreme Court which affect the public schools is relatively few. Within the subject areas of religion, segregation, and academic freedom, the number is even less. This chapter treats the cases which provide background information and principles preliminary to an examination of the public school cases decided by the Warren Court.

Presenting these subjects involves the discriminating selection of cases in two areas, religion and segregation. Several cases in religion touch more on parochial than on public schools; several cases in segregation deal with college and university education rather than with the elementary and secondary schools. However, these are included in this chapter for two major reasons. To exclude them would be to undertake a study without full benefit of an understanding of the significant issues surrounding the subsequent cases. Additionally, the Supreme Court has relied on these decisions for precedent as revealed by the opinions in later public school cases.

Religion

Since the Supreme Court first heard a case involving religion and the public schools, three areas of controversy have arisen. They have involved the expenditure of public funds for religious purposes, religious versus patriotic activities, and religious instruction. Each of these areas will be treated briefly.

Expenditure of funds. Government aid to parochial schools or to children in those schools was questioned very early in the twentieth century. The initial challenge came in *Quick Bear* v. *Leupp (1)* when Indians of the Sioux Tribe in South Dakota sought to enjoin payment of tribal funds to the Bureau of Catholic Indian Missions for Indian instruction on the reservation. An annual cost of $27,000 was to be paid to the Catholic Church under an arrangement worked out by the Commissioner of Indian Affairs.

Financial management of the Indian affairs was arranged through two treaties. Under the Treaty of 1868, the United States agreed to provide an annual appropriation of $225,000 if thirty children in the Sioux tribe would agree to attend school. A Treaty of 1899 created a permanent fund of $3,000,000 at 5 per cent interest, one-half being used for education. However, under an act of Congress in 1899, no money could be appropriated for education in any sectarian school.

Chief Justice Fuller heard an appeal from both parties. Leupp, the commissioner, had wanted to test the validity of the contract with the Catholic Church. The Indians sought an injunction to stop payment of funds to the Bureau of Catholic Missions and to enjoin the enforcement of a contract with a sectarian organization. Fuller upheld the commissioner's action in holding that the expenditure of funds was not in conflict with the 1899 act of Congress, since the funds actually belonged to the Indians, not to the federal government. The Chief Justice said:

> But we cannot concede the proposition that Indians cannot be allowed to use their own money to educate their children in the schools of their own choice because the Government is necessarily undenominational, as it cannot make any law respecting an establishment of religion or prohibiting the free exercise thereof (2).

Whereas *Quick Bear* concerned Congress and aid to religious schools, the next case questioning aid to parochial schools involved a state. In *Cochran v. Louisiana (3)* action was initiated to test the constitutionality of a state statute which provided for free textbooks from tax funds for children in nonpublic schools. It was alleged by the plaintiff that such action violated the Fourteenth Amendment. Chief Justice Hughes, speaking for the Court, held that such action was constitutionally permissible. He relied on the decision of the Louisiana Supreme Court, saying:

> One may scan the acts in vain to ascertain where any money is appropriated for the purchase of school books for the use of any church, private, sectarian or even public school. The appropriations were made for the specific purpose of purchasing school books for the use of the school children of the state, free of cost to them. It was for their benefit and the resulting benefit to the state that the appropriations were made. True, these children attend some school, public or private, the latter, sectarian or non-sectarian, and that the books are to be furnished them for their use, free of cost, whichever they attend. The schools, however, are not the beneficiaries of these appropriations. They obtain nothing from them, nor are they relieved of a single obligation, because of them. The school children and the state alone are the beneficiaries (4).

The "child benefit" theory has its origin in the *Cochran* decision. As applied here, the theory is that money used directly or indirectly for a child's education is an aid to the child and not to the school.

Since the school receives nothing, it does not stand to gain an advantage as does the child.

The theory was enlarged by the Supreme Court in 1947 in the *Everson* case (5). A closely-divided court in a 5-4 decision ruled that a local school district could reimburse parents of children attending parochial schools for certain school-related expenditures. The majority recognized that the tax money served the state and the pupils in a public welfare function through promotion of education without giving any aid to religion. Unlike *Cochran*, the *Everson* case clearly included parochial schools in the statute.

The school district of Ewing Township, acting under a New Jersey state statute, allowed the reimbursement. Everson, a taxpayer, filed suit in challenging the right of the school board to make such payments to parents. He cited both the First and the Fourteenth Amendments as being violated.

Justice Black, speaking for the majority, first clarified the meaning of the First Amendment. He held that a state could not set up a church nor aid any religion; neither could it force people to attend or to stay away from church. Further, he held that no tax could be used to support any religious activities. With such a standard as a guide, the Court held that Ewing Township had not violated the First Amendment.

Justice Jackson engaged in a strong dissent joined by Justice Frankfurter. They held that paying for transportation did not actually amount to rendering a public service. They objected to the discrimination of the statute which allowed reimbursement only to children in public or non-profit schools. This meant that, among the non-public schools, only the Catholic Church would benefit.

Justice Rutledge joined by Justice Burton dissented on the grounds that a more strict interpretation of the "wall of separation" between church and state should be maintained. They adhered to the principle that no form of public aid should be used to support religion. Under the Ewing program, the justices maintained that religion was being aided.

Religious versus patriotic activities. A case in the 1920's touched on the authority of the state to legislate wherein parochial schools are involved. In *Pierce* v. *Society of Sisters* (6) the Supreme Court was asked to rule on the constitutionality of a state statute which required that children attend a public school. Oregon passed a law, to become effective in 1926, that would require all children age eight to sixteen to attend a public school. Action challenging the law was initiated by the Society of Sisters, a parochial school, and Hill Military Academy, a private school. Both contended that the law was unreasonable; that, if enforced, it would destroy their business; and it interfered with parents' upbringing of children. Again, Justice McReynolds delivered the opinion. He said:

> The inevitable practical result of enforcing the Act under consideration would be destruction of appellees' primary schools, and perhaps all other primary schools for normal children within the state of Oregon. These parties are engaged in a kind of undertaking not inherently harmful, but long regarded as useful and meritorious. Certainly there is nothing in the present records to indicate that they have failed to discharge their obligations to patrons, students or the State. And there are no peculiar circumstances or present emergencies which demand extraordinary measures relative to primary education (7).

Further, McReynolds pointed out that:

> The child is not the mere creature of the State; those who nurture him and direct his destiny have the right, coupled with the high duty, to recognize and prepare him for additional obligations (8).

A more direct challenge to state action occurred in two flag salute cases. The Jehovah's Witnesses, a religious group, challenged a requirement that public school students be commanded to salute the flag at the opening of the school day. The Witnesses believed that such action amounted to the bowing before a graven image which the Bible forbids and is contrary to their beliefs.

The first of the two cases arose in the school district of Minersville, Pennsylvania (9), after the local school board passed a rule that all children salute the flag each day. Walter and Lillian Gobitis refused to execute the salute and were expelled from school. The father then sought to enjoin the school board from enforcing the requirement as a condition for school attendance. He held that such action was repugnant to the due process clause of the Fourteenth Amendment.

In an 8-1 decision, Justice Frankfurter, speaking for the majority, held the requirement to be valid. He based the decision on the fact that saluting the flag was a means of achieving national unity, and he felt the national interest to be paramount to one's individual freedom. The majority believed that patriotism could be instilled in the schools by requiring students to salute the flag. The opinion stated:

> "We live by symbols." The flag is the symbol of our national unity, transcending all internal differences, however large, within the framework of the Constitution. This Court has had occasion to say that ". . . the flag is the symbol of the Nation's power, the emblem of freedom in its truest, best sense. . . . it signifies government resting on the consent of the governed; liberty regulated by law; the protection of the weak against

BACKGROUND

the strong; security against the exercise of arbitrary power; and absolute safety for free institutions against foreign aggression *(10)*."

Frankfurter concluded that:

> ... the process may be utilized so long as men's right to believe as they please, to win others to their way of belief, and their right to assembly in their chosen places of worship for the devotional ceremonies of their faith, are all fully respected *(11)*.

In the case the Court did not decide specifically if the flag salute requirement contravened the First Amendment, although the justices did reaffirm that freedom of religion is not absolute. The Court grappled with the same issue three years later in *West Virginia* v. *Barnette (12)*.

Again, Jehovah's Witnesses brought suit, this time feeling more confident of winning their case. They had learned that some of the justices had had misgivings about their holding in *Gobitis*. This became evident in *Jones* v. *Opelika (13)* when Justices Black, Douglas, and Murphy indicated they should have voted for the plaintiffs in 1940. Further, a new justice came on the bench in early 1943 to replace Justice Byrnes. In the *Barnette* case the decision was 6-3, with Justice Jackson joining the majority and writing the opinion. For the first time in a public school case, the Supreme Court reversed itself.

The flag salute requirement in West Virginia was similar to the one in *Gobitis*, although two differences existed. Here, the ceremony resulted from a state, not a school board, action. Also, parents could be punished in West Virginia for their child's failure to salute the flag.

In overturning the statute, Justice Jackson answered initially Frankfurter's arguments in *Gobitis*. Here, Jackson made no distinction between what one believes and what one utters. He gave credence to the idea that patriotism cannot be legislated. He did not hold, however, that schools could not engage in flag salute exercises. He did rule that the ceremonies could not be required if persons objected due to religious scruples. He said:

> The case is made difficult not because the principles of its decision are obscure but because the flag involved is our own. Nevertheless, we apply the limitations of the Constitution with no fear that freedom to be intellectually and spiritually diverse or even contrary will disintegrate the social organization. To believe that patriotism will not flourish if patriotic ceremonies are voluntary and spontaneous instead of a compulsory routine is to make an unflattering estimate of the appeal of our institutions to free minds. ...
>
> If there is any fixed star in our constitutional constellation it is that no official, high or petty, can prescribe what shall be orthodox in politics, nationalism, religion, or other matters of opinion or force citizens to con-

fess by word or act their faith therein. If there are any circumstances which permit an exception, they do not now occur to us.

We think the action of the local authorities in compelling the flag salute and pledge transcends constitutional limitations on their power and invades the sphere of intellect and spirit which is the purpose of the First Amendment to our Constitution to reserve from all official control *(14)*.

Religious instruction. Religious instruction in the public schools has been a problem for school officials, an area of controversy for parents, and a litigious issue for the courts. Differences of opinion arise over what, if anything, of a religious nature should or should not be taught in the schools. Controversy has also developed over the relationship of cooperation between schools and sectarian groups wherein children are taught religion.

A case involving this subject reached the Supreme Court in 1948 *(15)*. It arose after the Champaign, Illinois, School District had devised plans for children to be taught religion in the public schools. This was actually the first case the Court decided which directly involved the teaching of religion in the public schools. The Court, in an 8-1 decision, declared the practice to be unconstitutional.

The plan in Champaign provided for religious instruction to be given in the local schools through a local organization, the Council on Religious Education. This group had in its membership persons from Catholic, Jewish, and Protestant faiths. Subject to local school supervision, the teachers selected by the Council went into the schools for forty-five minutes per week to offer instruction to students whose parents had requested the course. Separate classes were held for the three denominations. Students not participating went to another part of the school building for secular study.

Mrs. Vashti McCollum protested the practice and sought a remedy. She asked for a writ of mandamus to compel the school board to discontinue the religion classes. She contended that the practice violated the due process clause of the Fourteenth Amendment and the establishment clause of the First Amendment.

Justice Black, in speaking for the Court said that:

> The foregoing facts, without reference to others that appear in the record, show the use of tax-supported property for religious instruction and the close cooperation between the school authorities and the religious council in promoting religious education. The operation of the State's compulsory education thus assists and is integrated with the program of religious instruction carried on by separate religious sects. Pupils compelled by law to go to school for secular education are released in part from their legal duty upon the condition that they attend the religious classes. This is beyond all question a utilization of the tax-established and tax-supported public school system to aid religious groups to spread

their faith. And it falls squarely under the ban of the First Amendment *(16)*. . . .

The Court held the practice to be unconstitutional for two reasons. Justices saw that public, tax-supported buildings were being used to teach religious doctrines, and the school's compulsory machinery assisted the religious council. Those two guides did not, however, provide all solutions to the overall problem of religious instruction, for many school systems provided for the release of students from school during the day to attend religious centers for sectarian instruction. The question of the legality of "dismissed" time then arose in *Zorach* v. *Clauson (17)*.

A direct challenge was made in New York City where such a plan was in effect. Two taxpayers of the city alleged that the plan should be overturned for several reasons: (1) The school's influence and cooperation were being used to promote religious instruction. (2) Public school teachers aided the program by keeping attendance records. (3) Classroom activities were halted when the students in the religious classes left school.

Justice Douglas, speaking for the 6-3 majority, upheld the plan. He distinguished *Zorach* from *McCollum* in two ways. Whereas in *McCollum* the schools were used for instruction, there was no such problem in the instant case. Here, the school was not used to promote religion; rather, there was only cooperation between the institutions. Douglas stated:

> We are a religious people whose institutions presuppose a Supreme Being. We guarantee the freedom to worship as one chooses. We make room for as wide a variety of beliefs and creeds as the spiritual needs of man deem necessary. We sponsor an attitude on the part of government that shows no partiality to any one group and that lets each flourish according to the zeal of its adherents and the appeal of its dogma. When the state encourages religious instruction or cooperates with religious authorities by adjusting the schedule of public events to sectarian needs, it follows the best of our traditions. For it then respects the religious nature of our people and accommodates the public service to their spiritual needs *(18)*.

The same year that *Zorach* was decided, the Supreme Court received a case involving a related issue with a more detailed problem. *Doremus* v. *Board of Education (19)* was appealed to the Court to test the validity of a New Jersey statute requiring Bible reading in the classrooms. The act required the reading, without comment, of five verses of the Old Testament at the opening of the school day; it prohibited religious exercises other than Bible reading and the Lord's Prayer.

Two parents, identified as a taxpayer and a parent, sought to enjoin the enforcement of the act.

The case was rendered moot by the graduation of the only person who was complaining. The majority held that the appellant's interest as a taxpayer did not justify sufficient standing to sue. Further the justices noted that since the child involved had already graduated, no controversy existed. The Court declared that it would not render an advisory opinion.

On the basis of the religion cases affecting the public schools, the Supreme Court has provided several principles. It has held consistently that public funds may not be used to aid parochial schools; however, tax money may be spent to aid children in those schools. From this principle has come the "child benefit" theory which holds that the pupil may benefit from public taxes while the parochial school he attends will not. The benefit theory derived from two issues—the purchase of textbooks and the payment for pupil transportation. The application of this principle has not been examined nor extended by the Supreme Court beyond the two issues, although it leaves unanswered the question of under what circumstances the school does not benefit from money spent for the child.

The Supreme Court has also ruled that one is not required to attend a public school. It is recognized that parochial schools serve a useful purpose; furthermore, parents have some responsibility in preparing for their child's education. Placing the student in a non-public school is within the bounds of constitutional permissibility.

Patriotism cannot be legislated by requiring that school children salute the flag. A controversy over a compulsory flag salute in the school brought two cases before the Supreme Court. The second case overruled the earlier one, and the controlling principle holds that flag salute exercises may be held but not required if individuals object due to religious convictions.

Courses in religion may not be taught where school property and school funds are being used. The state is so involved in a religious activity that the establishment clause is violated. However, students may be released from school to receive religious instruction during the day, for this plan involves no more than cooperation between school and church.

Segregation

Segregation of the races in the public schools has as its legal background the *Plessy* v. *Ferguson (20)* decision by the United States Su-

BACKGROUND

preme Court in 1896. From that case came the principle of "separate but equal" schools which grew out of a larger problem, the power of a state to compel racial segregation in public transportation facilities.

The immediate case challenged a Louisiana statute requiring that races be segregated in railway transportation when Homer Plessy, seven-eighths white and one-eighth Negro, refused to ride in the section designated for Negroes. He contended that the statute violated the Thirteenth and Fourteenth Amendments. The Supreme Court did not consider the Thirteenth Amendment but based its decision on the Fourteenth. It upheld the statute as being reasonable and consistent with customs and tradition. The opinion stated:

> The object of the amendment was undoubtedly to enforce the absolute equality of the two races before the law, but in the nature of things it could not have been intended to abolish distinctions based on color, or to enforce social, as distinguished from political equality, or a commingling of the two races upon terms unsatisfactory to either. Laws permitting, and even requiring, their separation in places where they are liable to be brought into contact do not necessarily imply the inferiority of either race to the other, and have been generally, if not universally, recognized as within the competency of the state legislatures in the exercise of their police power (21).

The Court stated further that:

> ... the case reduces itself to the question whether the statute of Louisiana is a reasonable regulation, and with respect to this there must necessarily be a large discretion on the part of the legislature. In determining the question of reasonableness it is at liberty to act with reference to the established usages, customs and traditions of the people, and with a view to the promotion of their comfort, and the preservation of the public peace and good order. Gauged by this standard, we cannot say that a law which authorizes or even requires the separation of the two races in public conveyances is unreasonable or more obnoxious to the Fourteenth Amendment than the acts of Congress requiring separate schools for colored children in the District of Columbia, the constitutionality of which does not seem to have been questioned, or the corresponding acts of state legislatures (22).

Whereas Plessy argued that state-enforced segregation made the Negro feel inferior, the Court ruled that such state laws did not necessarily infer nor imply the inferiority of either race. Justice Brown, in the majority opinion, drew on *Roberts v. Boston*, a case decided by the Supreme Court of Massachusetts prior to the adoption of the Fourteenth Amendment. His answer to the argument was, "If this be so, it is not by reason of anything found in the act, but solely because the colored race chooses to put that construction upon it (23)."

Another of Plessy's arguments held that prejudice may be overcome by legislation. Justice Brown wrote in answer:

> If the two races are to be met upon terms of social equality, it must be the result of natural affinities, a mutual appreciation of each other's merits and a voluntary consent of individuals *(24)*.

The lone dissenter was Justice Harlan, grandfather of the present Justice Harlan. He wrote:

> Our Constitution is color-blind, and neither knows nor tolerates classes among citizens. In respect of civil rights, all citizens are equal before the law *(25)*.

In expressing very strong opposition to the majority decision, Harlan stated:

> In my opinion, the judgment this day rendered will, in time, prove to be quite as pernicious as the decision made by this tribunal in the *Dred Scott* case *(26)*.

Although the "separate but equal" doctrine became accepted, there is actually nothing in the *Plessy* opinion stating that segregation shall be permitted wherein facilities are equal. Further, the Court did not give any indication of what standards should be used to measure equality. The decision actually indicates a reluctance of the government to interfere in racial cases.

Only three years after *Plessy* was decided, the Court heard another segregation case, this time directly involving the public schools. In *Cumming* v. *Richmond County Board of Education (27)* the justices were asked to rule on the validity of an injunction which would close a white high school until a similar, separate school was provided for Negroes. The procedural question was thus no direct challenge to the *Plessy* doctrine; the Court's opinion offered no clarification of the separation principle.

The facts of the case showed that in Richmond County, Georgia, the only Negro high school, enrolling sixty students, was discontinued to permit the building to be converted into an elementary school to house three hundred pupils. The step was taken due to a lack of school funds. Within the county were three private schools charging the same tuition fee that Negroes paid for attending the public schools. In requesting the injunction, the Negroes alleged that inequality resulted from the county's failure to provide a high school for Negroes while the white people had theirs. In the oral argument the attorneys for the plaintiffs argued that separate schools were unconstitutional; however, the justices held in the opinion that such an allegation was given too late in the proceedings for the Court to act upon it.

BACKGROUND

The Court, speaking through Justice Harlan, was unanimous in refusing relief. The justices could find no evidence of racial discrimination. Further, they held that the relief requested was improper in that closing the white schools would not remedy the wrong suffered by the Negroes. Harlan reminded the plaintiffs that their case would have been stronger had they requested a mandamus to compel the opening of the Negro school.

Again, as in *Plessy*, the opinion shows that the Court recognized the authority of the state over education:

> We may add that while all admit that the benefits and burdens of public taxation must be shared by citizens without discrimination against any class on account of their race, the education of the people in schools maintained by state taxation is a matter of belonging to the respective States, and any interference on the part of Federal authority with the management of such schools cannot be justified except in the case of a clear and unmistakable disregard of rights secured by the supreme law of the land *(28)*.

No further elucidation of the "separate but equal" doctrine was discerned in the *Gong Lum* case *(29)*, decided twenty-seven years after *Cumming*. At issue here was the validity of the exclusion of a Chinese girl from a white school and her being placed in an all-Negro school. Martha Lum, a Chinese resident of Mississippi, objected to a school board order that she attend a Negro school since there was no school for her race. She contended that she should be assigned to the all-white school.

Chief Justice Taft wrote the Court's opinion, saying:

> The question here is whether a Chinese Citizen of the United States is denied equal protection of the laws when he is classed among the colored races and furnished facilities for education equal to that offered to all, whether white, brown, yellow or black. Were this a new question, it would call for very full argument and consideration, but we think that it is the same question which has been many times decided to be within the constitutional power of the state legislature to settle without intervention of the federal courts under the Federal Constitution *(30)*.

Taft reminded the plaintiff that "separate but equal" was still in effect:

> Had the petition alleged specifically that there was no colored school in Martha Lum's neighborhood to which she could conveniently go, a different question would have been presented, and this, without regard to the State Supreme Court's construction of the State Constitution as limiting the white schools provided for the education of children of the white or Caucasian race. But we do not find the petition to present such a situation *(31)*.

Gong Lum held that a state legislature may separate colored and white students; it may designate what persons shall be classed as colored. Whereas Mississippi had classified all non-whites as colored for purposes of school assignments, the Supreme Court recognized this as being valid. The Court recognized that, although a state has to furnish schools for all children, not all students have to be educated in the same school. Thus, the separation principle remained undisturbed.

Subsequent cases involving racial segregation before the Supreme Court prior to 1950 concerned the colleges and universities. In these cases the separation doctrine was scrutinized more carefully. In the *Gaines* case *(32)* of the 1930's, Chief Justice Hughes held that a Negro applicant must be offered the opportunity for a legal education in his home state. In the absence of a separate school for Negroes in Missouri, Lloyd Gaines had a right to attend a white law school. It was this case wherein the Court began to consider the "equal" part of the separation principle when the justices recognized that there are advantages of studying law in the state in which one lives and expects to practice. Similar facts prevailed in the *Sipuel* case *(33)* wherein the Court ordered the admission of a Negro to the University of Oklahoma Law School. The Court, in a brief *per curiam* opinion, recognized the appellant was qualified to enroll at the law school, its being the only one available in the state.

Following Sipuel's admission, the Oklahoma legislature revised the state statutes to allow Negroes to enroll at graduate institutions attended by whites if courses were not available at similar institutions for Negroes. The statute, however, provided for the segregation of Negroes within the white institution. McLaurin contested the discrimination and won before the Supreme Court *(34)*. The opinion of Chief Justice Vinson held that:

> The result is that appellant is handicapped in his pursuit of effective graduate instruction. Such restrictions impair and inhibit his ability to study, to engage in discussions and exchange views with other students, and, in general, to learn his profession *(35)*.

The opinion concluded that "Appellant, having been admitted to a state-supported graduate school, must receive the same treatment at the hands of the state as students of other races *(36)*."

The fourth of the graduate school cases, *Sweatt* v. *Painter (37)*, involved also the admission of a Negro at a law school, this one being at the University of Texas. Unlike the facts in *Gaines* and *Sipuel,* Texas had a separate law school for Negroes, but *Sweatt* applied at the University of Texas and was denied admission on racial grounds.

BACKGROUND

The question before the Court was the equality of the Negro law school with the one at the University. Sweatt's attorneys asked the Court to repudiate *Plessy* by overturning the "separate but equal" doctrine. Defense attorneys petitioned the Court to make a specific statement in recognition of the separate but equal principle in all areas of public education. The Court actually followed neither petition. It did recognize a substantial inequality in the two law schools, and, in so doing, dealt more specifically with intangible factors. The justices compared the two schools in terms of size of the faculty and student body, number of volumes in the library, court facilities, scholarship funds, and standing of the alumni. The Court, speaking through Chief Justice Vinson concluded:

> Whether the University of Texas Law School is compared with the original or the new law school for Negroes, we cannot find substantial equality in the educational opportunities offered white and Negro law students by the state. In terms of number of the faculty, variety of courses and opportunity for specialization, size of the student body, scope of the library, availability of law review and similar activities, the University of Texas Law School is superior. What is more important, the University of Texas Law School possesses to a far greater degree those qualities which are incapable of objective measurement but which make for greatness in a law school. Such qualities, to name but a few, include reputation of the faculty, experience of the administration, position and influence of the alumni, standing in the community, traditions and prestige. It is difficult to believe that one who had a free choice between these law schools would consider the question close (38).

The significance of the four university cases is manifest as one sees a gradual erosion of the separation doctrine. Both *Gaines* and *Sipuel* opened the way for Negroes to attend white institutions. *McLaurin* held that, once a school has been desegregated its facilities must be made available to all alike, its students must be accorded similar treatment. *Sweatt* expanded the holding in showing a segregated school to be unequal and in pointing out intangible factors as measurements of potential success. It was these cases which actually provided the springboard for an attack on segregation in the public elementary and secondary schools in a case to be heard by the Warren Court.

Academic Freedom

Cases before the Supreme Court questioning academic freedom are of recent origin. They have arisen out of a post-World War II scare over the possible infiltration of subversive persons in the school systems. To counter this threat, states and municipalities have adopted laws and ordinances designed to keep out undesirable persons and to insure that those currently employed will remain loyal. It is the legality of these measures that has been the basis for court litigation. The three cases here concern loyalty oaths and membership in subversive organizations.

Loyalty oaths. Two cases were decided by the United States Supreme Court in 1951 and 1952 on the question of the legality of loyalty oath laws. The Court sustained the validity of the oath requirement in *Garner* v. *Los Angeles (39)* but overturned an Oklahoma loyalty oath law in *Wieman* v. *Updegraff (40).*

In the *Garner* case an ordinance of the city of Los Angeles required that all city employees, including teachers, swear that, for the preceding five years, they had not advocated nor taught the overthrow of the government by force, violence, or other unlawful means. Further, the employee had to swear that, for the previous five years, he was not, is not, nor will not be a member of any party or organization engaging in such activities while in the employment of the city of Los Angeles. Also, the employee had to submit an affidavit listing past or present membership in the Communist Party.

The ordinance was challenged as being in violation of the Fourteenth Amendment and also as being an *ex post facto* law and a bill of attainder. The Court's majority held the action to be a reasonable measure of determining fitness rather than viewed it as a punishment for past activity.

Seven members of the Court held the affidavit requirement to be valid. They recognized that the Constitution does not forbid the city to require its employees to reveal past or present membership in the Communist Party. The justices did not decide if the city could discharge an employee who admitted membership in the party. Justice Clark's opinion stated:

> Past conduct may well relate to present fitness; past loyalty may have a reasonable relationship to present and future trust. Both are commonly inquired into in determining fitness for both high and low positions in private industry and are not less relevant in public employment *(41).*

Only five justices sustained the legality of the oath requirement while holding it was not a bill of attainder or *ex post facto* law. The majority held further that the oath did not deprive one of freedom of speech, assembly, and redress of grievances. Clark pointed out that the law provides standards of qualification and eligibility for persons in the public employ, and it does not penalize those for failure to meet these standards. The opinion indicated that government may protect the in-

BACKGROUND

tegrity and competency of those in public service and, to insure this, it may regulate an employee's political activities.

One year after *Garner* was decided the Court overturned a loyalty oath requirement in *Wieman* v. *Updegraff*. The case grew out of a 1951 statute of Oklahoma requiring all state employees to subscribe to a loyalty oath. One had to swear that he had not been a member of a subversive organization for the previous five years. Such organizations included any which advocated the overthrow of the government by force or violence, including the Communist Party, and any listed by the Attorney General as being subversive. Under terms of the statute, those subject to the oath would be required to execute it within thirty days of assuming employment. Thirteen employees of Oklahoma State Agricultural and Mechanical College tested the law by refusing to take the oath. They alleged that the oath law should be overturned because it was a bill of attainder and an *ex post facto* law, impaired the obligation of contracts with the state, and violated due process.

The Court was unanimous in striking down the law. Justice Clark's opinion held that it is denying one's constitutional rights to make membership, distinguished from knowing membership, a bar to public employment. The justices recognized that membership may be innocent; furthermore, some people have joined organizations only to withdraw later upon realizing their subversive character. Also, some organizations have been innocent when formed only to be infiltrated later by subversives.

Subversive organizations. In 1951 the Supreme Court was asked to rule on the constitutionality of a statute authorizing the dismissal of a teacher for membership in a subversive organization advocating the overthrow of the government. *Adler* v. *Board of Education (42)* attacked the Feinberg Law, a supplement to New York City's Civil Service Law, as being an *ex post facto* law and a bill of attainder. The Supreme Court upheld the statute.

The Feinberg Law, designed to keep subversives out of the school system, empowered the Board of Regents to adopt rules for the removal of violators. The Board did this by preparing a list of subversive organizations and making as subject for dismissal, any teacher holding membership in any of them. The proceedings allowed for a full hearing and the benefit of counsel. Adler, a public school teacher, and others sought to have the statute declared unconstitutional.

The Court rendered a 6-3 decision with Justice Minton writing the majority opinion. He said:

> A teacher works in a sensitive area in a schoolroom. There he shapes the attitude of young minds towards the society in which they live. In this, the state has a vital concern. It must protect the integrity of the schools. That the school authorities have the right and the duty to screen the officials, teachers, and employees as to their fitness to maintain the integrity of the schools as a part of ordered society, cannot be doubted. One's associates, past and present, as well as one's conduct, may properly be considered in determining fitness and loyalty *(43)*.

Justice Minton ruled that the plaintiffs could choose between employment in the schools and membership in a listed organization. Were they not to teach, they still would not be curbed in exercising their freedom of speech and assembly.

Justices Black, Frankfurter, and Douglas dissented. To Justice Douglas, the decision made "second class citizens" of teachers by denying them the freedom of thought and expression. He held that:

> ... the guilt of the teacher should turn on overt acts. So long as she is a law-abiding citizen, so long as her performance within the public school system meets professional standards, her private life, her political philosophy, her social creed should not be the cause of reprisals against her *(44)*.

The decisions of the limited number of cases involving a teacher's freedom indicate that one's rights are not absolute. In order to insure fitness for an employee, the employer may inquire into a person's previous activities, including memberships in subversive organizations. Further, an employer may require that a teacher subscribe to a loyalty oath. Limitations, however, cover both inquiries and oath laws. For one to be ineligible for employment due to membership in a subversive organization, he must have known at the time of his membership that it was subversive.

A loyalty oath requirement is legal if it is a determiner of fitness rather than a punishment for past conduct. The oath law may not be upheld if it attempts to include broad coverage of activities subject to proscription.

Teachers who work in the public schools may be screened concerning their past associations and conduct as a basis for determining fitness. That a teacher works in a setting wherein young minds are influenced makes him subject to close scrutiny by persons who employ him. This helps to protect the pupil, the school, and the state.

Notes to Chapter II

1. *Quick Bear v. Leupp*, 210 U.S. 50 (1908).
2. *Ibid.*, p. 81.

BACKGROUND

3. *Cochran* v. *Louisiana State Board of Education*, 281 U.S. 370 (1930).
4. *Ibid.*, p. 374.
5. *Everson* v. *Board of Education of Ewing Township*, 330 U.S. 1 (1947).
6. *Pierce* v. *Society of Sisters* (and Hill Military Academy), 268 U.S. 510 (1925).
7. *Ibid.*, p. 534.
8. *Ibid.*, p. 535.
9. *Minersville School District, Board of Education of Minersville School District et al.* v. *Gobitis et al.*, 310 U.S. 586 (1940).
10. *Ibid.*, p. 596.
11. *Ibid.*, p. 600.
12. *West Virginia State Board of Education et al.* v. *Barnette et al.*, 319 U.S. 624 (1943).
13. *Jones* v. *Opelika*, 316 U.S. 584 (1942).
14. *West Virginia, op. cit.*, p. 641.
15. *Illinois ex rel. McCollum* v. *Board of Education of School District No. 71, Champaign County, Illinois et al.*, 333 U.S. 203 (1948).
16. *Ibid.*, p. 209.
17. *Zorach et al.* v. *Clauson et al., Constituting the Board of Education of the City of New York et al.*, 343 U.S. 306 (1952).
18. *Ibid.*, p. 313.
19. *Doremus et al.* v. *Board of Education of the Borough of Hawthorne et al.*, 342 U.S. 429 (1952).
20. *Plessy* v. *Ferguson*, 163 U.S. 537 (1896).
21. *Ibid.*, p. 544.
22. *Ibid.*, p. 550.
23. *Ibid.*, p. 551.
24. *Ibid.*
25. *Ibid.*, p. 559.
26. *Ibid.*
27. *Cumming* v. *Richmond County Board of Education*, 175 U.S. 528 (1899).
28. *Ibid.*, p. 545.
29. *Gong Lum et al.* v. *Rice et al.*, 275 U.S. 78 (1927).
30. *Ibid.*, p. 85.
31. *Ibid.*, p. 84.
32. *Missouri ex rel. Gaines* v. *Canada, Registrar of the University of Missouri et al.*, 305 U.S. 337 (1938).
33. *Sipuel* v. *Board of Regents of the University of Oklahoma et al.*, 332 U.S. 631 (1948).
34. *McLaurin* v. *Oklahoma State Regents for Higher Education et al.*, 339 U.S. 637 (1950).
35. *Ibid.*, p. 641.
36. *Ibid.*, p. 642.
37. *Sweatt* v. *Painter et al.*, 339 U.S. 629 (1950).
38. *Ibid.*, p. 633.
39. *Garner* v. *Board of Public Works of Los Angeles et al.*, 341 U.S. 716 (1951).
40. *Wieman et al.* v. *Updegraff et al.*, 344 U.S. 183 (1952).
41. *Garner, op. cit.*, p. 720.
42. *Adler et al.* v. *Board of Education of the City of New York*, 342 U.S. 485 (1952).
43. *Ibid.*, p. 493.
44. *Ibid.*, p. 511.

Chapter III

RELIGION

Introduction

The First Amendment of the United States Constitution contains two clauses with respect to religion: "Congress shall make no law respecting an establishment of religion, or prohibiting the free exercise thereof...." This Amendment, adopted in 1791 along with the other first nine—generally called the Bill of Rights—, was originally restrictive only upon the federal government. The freedoms the amendments listed were not prohibitive of state action, and only the state's judgment prevented abuse.

Passage of the Fourteenth Amendment placed restrictions on state action. However, the Amendment did not originally extend the protection of the Bill of Rights to individuals from state invasion. A notable example is the case of *Cochran* v. *Louisiana State Board of Education (1)* in which a state statute was challenged for allowing free textbooks to be distributed to children in non-public as well as in public schools. Action was initiated under the due process clause of the Fourteenth Amendment rather than under one of the religion clauses of the First Amendment which would have challenged aid to religion or religious groups. Such recourse was not possible.

After 1940 the First Amendment began to restrict state action in matters of religion. This was made possible with the opinions of the Supreme Court that the fundamental freedoms of the First Amendment were incorporated into the due process clause of the Fourteenth Amendment as a protection against state action. The first religious case to declare this principle was *Cantwell* v. *Connecticut (2)*, when a unanimous Court overturned the conviction of a sect, the Jehovah's Witnesses, for allegedly disturbing the peace. In that decision Justice Roberts, speaking for the Court, said that the free exercise clause of the First Amendment was incorporated into the Fourteenth Amendment as a prohibition against state action. Seven years later Justice Black brought the establishment clause under the same amendment in *Everson* v. *Board of Education (3)*. Since 1947 there have been relatively few cases heard by the Supreme Court which involved religion in the public schools. Under Earl Warren's tenure as Chief Justice, eight cases have been decided. In the eight the major problem was that of treating the doctrine of separation of church and state. No problem would exist were the separation to be complete. If it were, there would be no religion in the schools and there would be no aid—either directly or indirectly—to parochial schools. However, there is no such thing as absolute separation. For example, the policeman investigates a burglary in a parochial school, and the fire department gives the same protection to a non-public as to a public school. On the other hand, tax money cannot be spent directly to aid a parochial school. The Court's function is to decide what constitutes separation and, after that determination, to resolve the specific issue. This function is not so easy as might appear, for it raises the question of where religious freedom collides with state action. The people of this country are committed to the principle of separation of church and state, but yet enjoy, to a considerable degree, freedom of religion.

Before 1952 the Supreme Court, through its decisions, had affected church-state relations in the public schools through these holdings: (1) A pupil may elect to attend a non-public school. (2) State action in allowing free textbooks and free bus transportation for children in parochial schools is constitutional. (3) A pupil may not be required to salute the flag if his religious conscience dictates otherwise. (4) Religious education within the public schools is not constitutional, although instruction in off-the-school centers during school hours is permissible.

In the cases decided prior to 1953 the Supreme Court had not given a definition of religion. In the religion decisions affecting public schools handed down by the Warren Court, no clear definition has been given either.

The two major decisions have one common question: the legality of devotional exercises within the schools. The first of the three decisions was given nine years after Warren was appointed as Chief Justice. That and the following cases involved one or both practices—the reading of the Bible and prayers at the opening of the school day. This chapter will present the background, the constitutional questions, the decisions, and then an analysis and interpretation of the principles involved in those opinions. In addition, it will treat the most recent decisions which touch on different aspects of maintaining the principle of separation of church and state.

The Cases

Case 1: Engel v. Vitale (1962). The first religion case *(4)* to be heard by the Warren Court involved the constitutionality of the use of a prayer in the schools of New York.

In a study of moral education in the public schools of that state, the Board of Regents in its 1951 "Statement on Moral and Spiritual Training in the Schools" recommended that the following prayer be used:

> Almighty God, we acknowledge our dependence upon Thee, and we beg Thy blessings upon us, our parents, our teachers and our country *(5)*.

The state authorities made the prayer doubly optional—at the option of the school board and at the option of the parents.

The Board of Education of Union Free School District Number 9, New Hyde Park, New York, directed that the prayer be used in the school's opening exercises. Initially, the local school board made no provision for excusing students from the classroom while the prayer was being recited.

Five parents representing ten school children in the district brought suit, protesting that the prayer was contrary to the beliefs, religion, or religious practices of them and their children. The religious affiliation of the parents included Jewish, Ethical Culture Society, and one nonbeliever. These parents maintained that the prayer imposed some coercion on their children. They insisted that state authorization of the prayer for use within the school district contravened the establishment clause of the First Amendment.

Before the case reached the United States Supreme Court, the plaintiffs lost in each of the lower courts. The New York State Supreme Court, although recognizing the religious nature of the prayer, refused a plea to ban its recitation. A branch of the New York Appellate Division sustained the decision as did New York's highest court.

The New York Court of Appeals upheld the decision of the trial court in allowing the prayer to be said so long as the school did not compel any pupil to recite it if her or his parents objected. The five complaining parents then took their appeal to the United States Supreme Court. In a decision handed down on June 23, 1962, Justice Black, speaking for the Court, held that a statute authorizing the daily recitation of a prayer was in violation of the First Amendment. Justice Douglas wrote a concurring opinion while Justice Stewart dissented. Although he heard the argument, Justice Frankfurter did not participate in the decision. Justice White took no part in either the discussion or the decision.

In arriving at the Court's decision, Black relied on a study of history rather than an examination of precedents of previous Court opinions. He cited England's adoption of the Book of Common Prayer as being one reason for colonists' coming to America. He also referred to the fight led by Thomas Jefferson and James Madison who opposed religious establishment. Next, Black reviewed the historical background which led to the adoption of the Constitution and later the addition of the First Amendment. In asserting that government cannot control what prayers the American people say, Black added:

> Under that Amendment's prohibition against governmental establishment of religion, as reinforced by the provisions of the Fourteenth Amendment, government in this country, be it state or federal, is without power, to prescribe by law any particular form of prayer which is to be used as an official prayer in carrying on any program of governmentally sponsored religious activity (6).

Black reviewed the allegations of the plaintiffs who insisted that the prayer violated the establishment clause. He said:

> We agree with that contention since we think that the constitutional prohibition against laws respecting an establishment of religion must at least mean that in this country it is no part of the business of government to compose official prayers for any group of the American people to recite as a part of a religious program carried on by government (7).

Black's majority opinion sought to make clear that the Court's holding in restricting governmental involvement in religion was in no way intended to imply that the Court had a disrespect for religion. Black added:

> It has been argued that to apply the Constitution in such a way as to prohibit state laws respecting an establishment of religious services in public schools is to indicate a hostility toward religion or toward prayer. Nothing, of course, could be more wrong. The history of man is inseparable from the history of religion (8).

Public schools have a responsibility, Black indicated, to develop citizens for their good and for the good of the state. Since the school is an agency of the state, the schools must be neutral in religious activity. The Court's position held:

> It is neither sacrilegious nor antireligious to say that each separate government in this country should stay out of the business of writing or sanctioning official prayers and leave that purely religious function to the

people themselves and to those the people choose to look to for religious guidance *(9)*.

The real issue, according to Justice Douglas, in his concurring opinion, was whether the government could finance a religious exercise. After recognizing that, although a very short time was consumed for recitation of the prayer, Douglas concluded:

> Yet for me the principle is the same, no matter how briefly the prayer is said, for in each of the instances given the person praying is a public official on the public payroll, performing a religious exercise in a governmental institution *(10)*.

Justice Stewart registered the sole dissent. He took issue with the holding of the justices in the majority that the prayer established a religion. He wrote:

> The court does not hold, nor could it, that New York has interfered with the free exercise of anybody's religion. For the state courts have made clear that those who object to reciting the prayer must be entirely free of any compulsion to do so, including any "embarrassments and pressures. . . ." But the Court says that in permitting school children to say this simple prayer, the New York authorities have established "an official religion *(11)*."

Stewart then disagreed with the majority when he asserted that those students who wished to say a prayer should be permitted to do so.

Stewart then attacked Black's reference to the Book of Common Prayer as being irrelevant to the case. What is appropriate, he indicated, is a history of the traditions of the American people. He also took issue with Black's concern over an established church, maintaining that no such problem existed in this country.

Case 2: Abington v. Schempp (1963). The year following the Engel decision the Supreme Court gave a ruling on the constitutionality of reading the Bible and praying the Lord's Prayer in *School District of Abington Township v. Schempp (12)*. This decision had considerable impact on the public schools, as it affected possibly 40 per cent of the nation's school children *(13)*.

The decision joined two cases before the Court *(14)*. When the Schempp family instituted court proceedings in 1958, it marked the first time that Bible-reading had been challenged in a federal court *(15)*. The Schempp family objected to a 1949 statute of Pennsylvania requiring that at least ten verses of scripture be read in the public schools, without comment, at the opening of each day.

The Bible was read over the intercommunication system by students enrolled in a class in broadcasting. Following the reading of the Bible, the teachers asked that all students stand and recite the Lord's Prayer.

Although the Pennsylvania statute did not specify which version of the Bible to use, evidence indicated that a Protestant one was always followed. Moreover, local school officials bought copies of the King James version to be made available to the teachers. Pupils could, nevertheless, read from the Roman Catholic or Jewish versions if they chose. Reciting the Lord's Prayer was optional but taken for granted. No provision was made in the original statute for excusing pupils who did not want to participate. Any teacher who did not comply with the ruling could be discharged.

Parents of the Schempp children did not ask that their children be excused from the exercises, as they felt that this would harm relationships with the children's teachers and fellow classmates. One of the Schempp children refused to stand for the Lord's Prayer, instead, he studied the Koran while the Bible was read over the public-address system. He was first disciplined by being stationed in an office during the opening exercises; later he was returned to his homeroom over his protest.

Case 3: Murray v. Curlett (1963). The other case, *Murray et al. v. Curlett et al., Constituting the Board of Commissioners of Baltimore City (16),* involved related but different facts. Mrs. Madalyn Murray and her son Bill, avowed atheists, challenged a 1905 ordinance of Baltimore which required that a chapter of the Bible be read and/or the Lord's Prayer be recited daily. At the time that the Murrays began their fight there was no provision for excusing children from the exercises. The rule was later amended to permit children to leave the room upon the written excuse of their parents.

Mrs. Murray and her son protested that the exercises were in violation of the First and Fourteenth Amendments. They held that the schools were establishing religion and thus destroying Bill's religious freedom. School officials made no concessions, and Bill became a truant for eighteen days. Upon his return ensuing negotiations permitted him to remain outside the room during the morning devotions. Mrs. Murray continued her battle by taking the case to court. Unlike the *Schempp* trial, no testimony was taken. The Baltimore School Board demurred but insisted that the Murray allegations were insufficient to grant the family relief.

The two cases were argued before the Supreme Court on successive days and then joined for the Court's consideration and opinion. On

June 17, 1963, the Court held that both practices abridged the establishment clause of the First Amendment. This decision, unlike *Engel*, produced three concurring opinions; Justices Douglas, Brennan, and Goldberg, joined by Harlan, concurred with the result in separate opinions. As in *Engel*, Justice Stewart dissented.

Writing for the majority, Justice Clark dealt with the Court's concept of the establishment clause. He recognized that the Constitution prohibits a law establishing a religion; it also prohibits a state from compelling a religious belief. Since the state is barred from establishing a religion or a religious belief, then the school, as an agency of the state, is similarly restrained. Since the state has no religion, the school likewise has none and cannot include religion in its curriculum.

Clark then touched on the concept of the First Amendment and the extent of its reach. He wrote:

> First, this Court has decisively settled that the First Amendment's mandate that "Congress shall make no law respecting an establishment of religion, or prohibiting the free exercise thereof" has been made wholly applicable to the states by the Fourteenth Amendment. . . . In a series of cases . . . the Court has repeatedly reaffirmed that doctrine, and we do so now. . . .
> Second, this Court has rejected unequivocally the contention that the establishment clause forbids only governmental preference of one religion over another. . . . The same conclusion has been firmly maintained ever since that time, . . . and we reaffirm it now.
> While none of the parties to either of these cases has questioned these basic conclusions of the Court, both of which have been long established, recognized and consistently reaffirmed, others continue to question their history, logic and efficacy. Such contentions, in the light of the consistent interpretation in cases of this Court, seem entirely untenable and of value only as academic exercises *(17)*.

The Court included a test to determine the constitutionality of a law requiring religious exercises. Justice Clark wrote:

> The test may be stated as follows: what are the purpose and the primary effect of the enactment? If either is the advancement or inhibition of religion then the enactment exceeds the scope of legislative power as circumscribed by the Constitution. That is to say that to withstand the strictures of the Establishment Clause there must be a secular legislative purpose and a primary effect that neither advances nor inhibits religion. . . . The Free Exercise Clause, likewise considered many times here, withdraws from legislative power, state and federal, the exertion of any restraint on the free exercise of religion. Its purpose is to secure religious liberty in the individual or prohibiting any invasions thereof by civil authority *(18)*.

The opening exercise is a religious ceremony and was designed by the state for that purpose, so ruled the Supreme Court in agreeing with the trial court of Pennsylvania. There was no similar finding in the

Maryland case. The Supreme Court did observe, however, that the program had a secular purpose in promoting moral values. Clark said about this:

> But even if its purpose is not strictly religious, it is sought to be accomplished through readings, without comment, from the Bible. Surely the place of the Bible as an instrument of religion cannot be gainsaid, and the State's recognition of the pervading religious character of the ceremony is evident from the rule's specific permission of the alternative use of the Catholic Douay version as well as the recent amendment permitting non-attendance at the exercises. None of these factors is consistent with the contention that the Bible is here used either as an instrument for nonreligious moral inspiration or as a reference for the teaching of secular subjects *(19)*.

The Court concluded that in both cases the laws require religious exercises held in violation of the rights of the parents and school children who protested.

For those who contended that the exercises were only minor encroachments on the First Amendment, Clark gave this answer:

> Further, it is no defense to urge that the religious practices here may be relatively minor encroachments on the First Amendment. The breach of neutrality that is today a trickling stream may all too soon become a raging torrent and, in the words of Madison, "it is proper to take alarm at the first experiment on our liberties *(20)*."

Another contention was that the removal of religious exercises from the schools would establish a religion of secularism. Clark responded to that:

> We agree of course that the State may not establish a "religion of secularism" in the sense of affirmatively opposing or showing hostility to religion, thus "preferring those who believe in no religion over those who do not believe." ... We do not agree, however, that this decision in any sense has that effect *(21)*.

A third contention was that all religious study might be removed from the schools. Clark made a distinction between the religious exercises and the study of religion, holding that the study of religion in history is not affected by this decision.

The Court reaffirmed that majority rule is not in effect in matters of religion. The individual may elect to worship or not worship, to believe or not believe as he wishes. Rule by the majority in a religious issue would, in effect, be the establishment of a state church. Clark elaborated:

> Finally, we cannot accept that the concept of neutrality, which does not permit a State to require a religious exercise even with the consent of

the majority of those affected, collides with the majority's right to free exercise of religion. While the Free Exercise Clause clearly prohibits the use of state action to deny the rights of free exercise to anyone, it has never meant that a majority could use the machinery of the State to practice its beliefs *(22)*.

Justice Douglas's opinion overruled the devotional exercises on two counts—the school as a medium of the state conducting a religious exercise and the use of state funds to promote the exercises. Douglas wrote:

> In each case the State is conducting a religious exercise; and, as the Court holds, that cannot be done without violating the "neutrality" required of the State by the balance of power between individual, church and state that has been struck by the First Amendment. But the Establishment Clause is not limited to precluding the State itself from conducting religious exercises *(23)*.

In recognizing that public funds were being expended for the promotion of a religious exercise, Douglas held that:

> Such contributions may not be made by the State even in a minor degree without violating the Establishment Clause. It is not the amount of public funds expended; as this case illustrates, it is the use to which public funds are put that is controlling *(24)*.

Justice Brennan wrote a lengthy opinion—over twice as long as the majority, dissenting, and other concurring opinions combined. Brennan first traced the Court's decisions involving the religious cases and the First Amendment. Next, he considered the intention of the framers of the Constitution. He found it impossible to rely solely upon them for guidelines in fashioning his opinion. He noted the great change in the educational systems in this country since the adoption of the First Amendment. He also observed the heterogeneity of the religious population as being much more diverse today than formerly.

In applying his background study to the Bible reading case, Brennan stated:

> Daily recital of the Lord's Prayer and the reading of the passages of Scripture are quite as clearly breaches of the command of the Establishment Clause as was the daily use of the rather bland Regent's Prayer in the New York public schools. Indeed, I would suppose that, if anything, the Lord's Prayer and the Holy Bible are more clearly sectarian, and the present violations of the First Amendment consequently more serious *(25)*.

Goldberg, in his concurrence joined by Justice Harlan, found it difficult to delineate the relationship of government and religion. He recognized the role of religion among the people of this country saying:

Neither the state nor this Court can or should ignore the significance of the fact that a vast portion of our people believe in and worship God and that many of our legal, political and personal values derive historically from religious teachings (26).

Justice Stewart dissented; moreover, he would have remanded the two cases for more evidence. He noted that neither party attacked the devotional exercises as being "establishments"; rather, the two families had asserted that their personal liberties had been violated. Stewart accused the Court majority of using "mechanistic" applications of the metaphor, "wall of separation."

After tracing some earlier cases heard by the Court involving religion, Stewart analyzed the neutrality aspect of the religious exercises. He wrote:

It might also be argued that parents who want their children exposed to religious influences can adequately fulfill that wish off school property and outside school time. With all its surface persuasiveness, however, this argument seriously misconceives the basic constitutional justification for permitting the exercises at issue in these cases. For a compulsory state educational system so structures a child's life that if religious exercises are held to be an impermissible activity in schools, religion is placed at an artificial and state-created disadvantage. Viewed in this light, permission of such exercises for those who want them is necessary if the schools are truly to be neutral in the matter of religion. And a refusal to permit religious exercises thus is seen, not as the realization of state neutrality, but rather as the establishment of a religion of secularism, or at the least, as government support of the beliefs of those who think that religious exercises should be conducted only in private (27).

Next, Stewart treated the element of coercion. It was on this that Stewart felt the real issue turned.

In other words, the question presented here is not whether exercises such as those at issue here are constitutionally compelled, but rather whether they are constitutionally invalid. And that issue, in my view, turns on the question of coercion.
It is clear that the dangers of coercion involved in the holding of religious exercises in a schoolroom differ qualitatively from those presented by the use of similar exercises or affirmations in ceremonies attended by adults. Even as to children, however, the duty laid upon government in connection with religious exercises in the public schools is that of refraining from so structuring the school environment as to put any kind of pressure on a child to participate in those exercises; it is not that of providing an atmosphere in which children are kept scrupulously insulated from any awareness that some of their fellows may want to open the school day with prayer, or of the fact that exist in our pluralistic society differences of religious belief. . . .
. . . .
It may well be, as has been argued to us, that even the supposed benefits to be derived from non-coercive religious exercises in public schools are incommensurate with the administrative problems which they

would create. The choice involved, however, is one for each local community and its school board, and not for this Court. For, as I have said, religious exercises are not constitutionally invalid if they simply reflect differences which exist in the society from which the school draws its pupils. They become constitutionally invalid only if their administration places the sanction of secular authority behind one or more particular religious or irreligious beliefs *(28)*.

Finally, Stewart would remand the cases for additional findings. He indicated the following lack of evidence to support his claim: (1) Both cases involved provisions allowing students to be excused from the exercises. (2) There was no evidence of coercion on any student not wanting to participate. (3) No evidence was taken in the *Murray* case. (4) The *Schempp* case showed a subjective guess by a parent about what he thought might happen if his children were excused. (5) Since Mr. Schempp had made no request for children to be excused, there is no evidence of what might have happened nor is there evidence of arrangements the school administrators could have made to free the children from pressures. (6) There were no district court findings in the *Schempp* case.

Case 4: Chamberlin v. Dade County (1964). A case to come before the courts in America to include many of the religious exercises the public schools engage in was *Chamberlin v. Dade County (29).* Action under this case was brought before the Supreme Court to challenge Bible reading, prayer, Christmas celebrations, religious symbols, baccalaureate programs, a religious census among pupils, and a religious test for teachers—all in the schools. The activities were based on a Florida statute that required Bible reading in the schools:

Whereas it is in the interest of good moral training, of a life of honorable thought and good citizenship that the public school children should have lessons of morality brought to their attention during their school days *(30)*.

Parents of varying religious backgrounds—agnostic, Jewish, and Unitarian—brought action in protest of the exercises under the statute. They protested that all of the practices were unconstitutional. Before the issue was finally settled, the case had gone through several courts, including two appearances in the United States Supreme Court.

In the Florida Circuit Court for Dade County the judge, for the first time in any American court, banned plays in the public schools built around Christmas and the birth of Christ and around Easter and the crucifixion of Christ. The judge held that such plays constituted religious teaching. He also banned religious movies and sectarian comments on the Bible. He upheld Bible reading and prayers. He also upheld a religious test for teachers wherein a prospective teacher is asked, "Do you believe in God?"

Before the Florida Supreme Court for the first time in 1962, the justices enjoined some of the practices while upholding others. The court did not approve the following: sectarian comments on the Bible by teachers, use of the school premises after school for Bible instruction, showing of religious films, and observance of Christmas, Easter, and Hanukkah as religious holidays. The justices upheld reading of the Bible, distributing sectarian literature, praying the Lord's Prayer and other prayers, singing religious hymns, displaying religious symbols, holding baccalaureate services, conducting a religious census among pupils, and using the religious test for teachers.

The state supreme court took note of decisions involving religion that were heard in the United States Supreme Court, but disagreed with the higher court's analysis of the First Amendment; moreover, the justices accepted minority opinions as bases for their interpretation. The justices adopted a different line of philosophy in upholding exercises when they saw religious activities as being one answer to the country's struggle with Communism. The court's opinion held:

> For all practical purposes there are now in the world just two forms of government, loosely denominated Democracy and Communism. The vital difference between the two is that the Democracies accept religion and guarantee its free exercise, in one form or another, as part of the day to day lives of their people, whereas Communism has banished religion, except as it may be bootlegged in the dark and inhospitable corners. . . . Typical of the American custom of meeting the other side more than half way, is the paradox of the appellee school board insuring the free exercise of religion while, by mandatory statute, it must teach the history, doctrines, objectives and techniques of Communism. Thus the school board affords the atheists the freedom of hearing or not hearing the Bible read while it requires that all students, without choice, be taught the facts of Communism, the antithesis of the Bible *(31)*.

On appeal to the United States Supreme Court, the case was disposed of summarily by the justices *(32)*. They vacated judgment and remanded the case to the Florida Supreme Court for further consideration in light of the *Schempp* decision issued the same day.

When the case returned to the state court, the appellants asked if Dade County violated the United States Constitution through five practices: (1) reading Bible verses in assembly and in classrooms, (2) reciting the Lord's Prayer and other sectarian prayers, (3) holding baccalaureate services, (4) conducting a religious census among pupils, and (5) conducting a religious test as a qualification for teacher employment. The judge, taking note of the United States Supreme Court order, maintained that the facts of this case were dissimilar from the *Schempp* case. He held that the Florida statute was founded on secular rather than sectarian considerations and thus was inoffensive to the establishment clause.

As they turned to answering the constitutionality of the five practices, the justices dealt only with problems three, four, and five. The men took note that only the high school has a baccalaureate service. Since all the protesting pupils except one were enrolled in elementary or in junior high school, the complainants had no standing to sue. The justices also noted that no religious census had been taken. There was no indication that the children had been questioned or that they had supplied any information pertinent to a religious census. Furthermore, since none of the appellants taught school, the question of the constitutionality of a religious test for teachers would not be considered by the court. The justices reaffirmed their position that they do not render advisory opinions.

On its second appearance before the United States Supreme Court, the justices issued a brief *per curiam* opinion on June 1, 1964. They held that, following the *Schempp* decision, devotional Bible reading by statute and the recitation of prayers are unconstitutional. Concerning the other three issues, the justices dismissed the appeal for lack of federal questions.

Case 5: Stein v. *Oshinsky (1965).* An appeal was filed with the Court to act on a school's prohibiting the recitation of voluntary prayers in a New York City school *(33).* Without giving a reason, the justices unanimously agreed not to grant *certiorari.* Parents of children enrolled in a public nursery school in Queens brought action to enjoin the principal from preventing the children saying the following prayer:

> God is great, God is good
> And we thank Him for our food, Amen.

The suit also protested the prohibition of the following prayer's being said:

> Thank you for the world so sweet
> Thank you for the food we eat
> Thank you for the birds that sing
> Thank you God for everything.

The principal had issued the ban in September 1962, following the *Schempp* decision. He contended that the prayers had been taught to the children by the teachers.

Case 6: Board v. *Allen (1968).* Just before adjourning for the summer in 1968, the Court handed down two opinions touching on the relationship of church and state. The first, *Board v. Allen (34)* was a challenge to a law of the state of New York that required local school officials to lend textbooks at no cost to students enrolled in grades seven through twelve, public and non-public schools. Speaking for the majority of the Court, Justice White upheld the practice. Justices Fortas, Black, and Douglas dissented. Justice Harlan concurred with the majority in a separate opinion.

Litigation was predicated on an action by the state legislature which amended an earlier statute authorizing school boards to designate, purchase, and then sell or rent books to public school students. The 1965 action enlarged the act to include distribution of texts to children in parochial schools. This was challenged by members of school boards in two counties as being in violation of both the New York State and federal constitutions.

Justice White relied on Court holdings of the past forty-three years to support the majority's holding. The controlling precedent was *Everson* which had sustained payment of tax funds for transportation of children to parochial schools. The Court recognized that often the line separating church and state is one of degree. The real test in this case was based on Clark's "purpose and primary effect" of *Schempp*. Justice White thus reasoned: (1) The New York statute neither advances nor inhibits religion. (2) Books are not actually furnished schools; they are provided for children, and it is they and their parents who benefit. (3) Ownership of the books resides in the state. The public school authorities, in fact, approve the selection of the books.

The appellants had maintained that books would be used to teach religion. Relying on *Pierce*, the Court recognized the value of having parochial schools and of the two goals they pursue: religious instruction and secular education. White stated further:

> Underlying these cases and underlying also the legislative judgments that have preceded the court decisions has been a recognition that private education has played and is playing a significant and valuable role in raising national levels of knowledge, competence, and experience *(35)*.

Justice Fortas attacked the cooperative program of the state. He held that parochial school officials actually selected the texts even though public school authorities approved them. He held:

> This program in its unconstitutional features, is hand-tailored to satisfy the specific needs of sectarian schools. Children attending such schools are given *special* books—books selected by the sectarian authorities. How can this be other than the use of public money to aid those sectarian establishments *(36)*?

Fortas would also distinguish between such public services as police and fire protection and books, holding that the former are not selected for a given religious group.

In dissenting also, Justice Black held that the New York law "is a flat, flagrant, open violation of the First and Fourteenth Amendments which together forbid Congress or state legislatures to enact any law 'respecting an establishment of religion *(37).*' " He held that tax support for such books places the state squarely in a religious activity.

Black distinguished the present case from *Everson,* stating:

> That law [*Everson*] did not attempt to deny the benefit of its general terms to children of any faith going to any legally authorized school. Thus, it was treated in the same way as a general law paying the streetcar fare *of all school children,* or a law providing midday lunches for all children or all school children, or a law to provide police protection for children going to and from school, or general laws to provide police and fire protection for buildings, including, of course, churches and church school buildings, as well as others.
>
> Books are the most essential tool of education since they contain the resources of knowledge which the educational process is designed to exploit. In this sense it is not difficult to distinguish books, which are the heart of any school, from bus fares, which provide a convenient and helpful general public transportation service *(38).*

Black then saw the possible potential reach of this law:

> [It] makes but a small inroad and does not amount to complete establishment of religion. But that is no excuse for upholding it. It requires no prophet to foresee that on the argument used to support this law others could be upheld providing for state or federal government funds to erect religious buildings or to erect the buildings themselves, to pay the salaries of the religious school teachers, and finally to have the sectarian religious groups cease to rely on voluntary contributions of members of their sects while waiting for the Government to pick up all the bills for the religious schools *(39).*

In his dissent, Justice Douglas indicated that parochial school officials do have some discretion in determining what books will be selected.

Like Black, Douglas also distinguished between aid for transportation and aid for books. He said:

> [T]here is nothing ideological about a bus. There is nothing ideological about a school lunch, nor a public nurse, nor a scholarship. The constitutionality of such public aid to students in parochial schools turns on considerations not present in the textbook case. The textbook goes to the very heart of education in a parochial school. It is the chief, although not solitary, instrumentality for propagating a particular religious creed or faith *(40).*

Case 7: Flast v. *Cohen (1968).* In the second opinion, in an 8-1 decision, the Court altered a 45-year-old doctrine holding that a federal taxpayer lacks standing to challenge the expenditure of federal funds. In *Flast* v. *Cohen (41)* the justices held that an individual may bring suit if he feels the legislation is in violation of the First Amendment prohibition of an establishment of religion or an abridgment of free exercise.

Chief Justice Warren wrote the majority opinion; Justices Douglas, Stewart, and Fortas wrote concurring opinions. Harlan dissented.

In this case the appellants registered their complaints solely as taxpayers who were in opposition to expenditure of tax funds under Titles II and III of the Elementary and Secondary Education Act. Provision was made under the act to finance instruction in reading, arithmetic, and other subjects in parochial schools as well as to purchase books and other instructional materials for such schools.

The government sought to dismiss the complaint on the ground that appellants lacked standing to sue, a position consistent with *Frothingham* v. *Mellon (42).* Without specifically overruling this case, the Court opened the way for individuals to sue. It is expected now that the Supreme Court will hear one or more suits challenging the constitutionality of cooperative programs under the Elementary and Secondary Education Act.

Warren maintained that the *Frothingham* opinion was not clear with respect to its intended scope. He sought to allay the fears of persons who might see a rash of suits brought by taxpayers by holding that it is possible for one to bring a class action suit.

Reminding the parties to the case that the federal courts are restricted to "cases" and "controversies," Warren proceeded to define the limits of a justiciable case. He held that the Supreme Court does not decide cases which resolve political questions, render advisory opinions, treat a moot issue, or hear an appeal by an individual lacking standing.

It was the question of standing to sue with which this case dealt. Warren stated:

> The fundamental aspect of standing is that it focuses on the party seeking to get his complaint before a federal court and not on the issues he wishes to have adjudicated *(43).*

Having held that Article III of the Constitution does not prohibit challenges to federal spending programs, Warren then sought to resolve the question as to the conditions under which one's personal interest in a program may permit suit. In order for one to have the necessary standing to sue, Warren held that the individual must meet two requirements:

> First, the taxpayer must establish a logical link between that status and the type of legislative enactment attacked. . . . Secondly, the taxpayer must establish a nexus between that status and the precise nature of the constitutional infringement alleged. Under this requirement, the taxpayer must show that the challenged enactment exceeds specific constitutional limitations imposed upon the exercise of the congressional taxing and spending power and not simply that the enactment is generally beyond the powers delegated to Congress by Art. I, Sec. 8 *(44)*.

Warren held that the appellants in this case had satisfied both claims. He referred in particular to the second link, that taxing power could conceivably be used to favor one religion or to support religion in general.

In distinguishing *Flast* from *Frothingham*, Warren held that the former met both requirements; the latter met only the first requirement.

Case 8: Epperson v. Arkansas (1968). Academic freedom clashing with religious theories resulted in the Supreme Court ruling on the validity of an anti-evolution law. The appeal challenged a 1928 act of Arkansas which prohibited instructors in public schools and colleges from teaching that man evolved from other species of life. Teaching or adopting a textbook that included such information was considered a misdemeanor, with the person in question subject to dismissal.

The *Epperson* case *(45)* arose at Central High School, Little Rock, when Susan Epperson, a biology teacher, initiated action to declare the statute void. Miss Epperson had been issued a text containing a chapter treating the Darwinian theory of evolution. The book had been adopted by the school system prior to the second year that Miss Epperson was to teach at Central School.

Before the Supreme Court, the justices agreed that the statute could not be sustained. Justice Fortas wrote the majority opinion, and there were three concurring opinions by Justices Black, Harlan, and Stewart.

In arriving at the Court's decision, Justice Fortas first raised the question of the vagueness of the statute. He could not decide if the act forbade explaining the theory or if it merely prohibited teaching that the theory is true. He concluded that the question of vagueness could not be the essential element in deciding the case, adding:

> the law must be striken because of its conflict with the constitutional prohibition of state laws respecting an establishment of religion or prohibiting the free exercise thereof. The overriding fact is that Arkansas'

law selects from the body of knowledge a particular segment which it proscribes for the sole reason that it is deemed to conflict with a particular religious doctrine; that is, with a particular interpretation of the Book of Genesis by a particular religious group *(46)*.

For precedent the opinion relied on previous Court decisions covering questions of both religion and academic freedom. However, to the justices, the law was an abridgment of the establishment-of-religion clause of the First Amendment.

There is and can be no doubt that the First Amendment does not permit the state to require that teaching and learning must be tailored to the principles or prohibitions of any religious sect or dogma *(47)*.

Fortas added:

These precedents inevitably determine the result in the present case. The State's undoubted right to prescribe the curriculum for its public schools does not carry with it the right to prohibit, on pain of criminal penalty, the teaching of a scientific theory or doctrine where that prohibition is based upon reasons that violate the First Amendment. It is much too late to argue that the State may impose upon the teachers in its schools any conditions that it chooses, however restrictive they may be of constitutional guarantees *(48)*.

The Court recognized that the state had approved the act during a time when fundamental thinking was very evident in the country. Arkansas had sought to prohibit the teaching of evolution because such a doctrine clashed with the thinking of some persons who rely exclusively on a literal interpretation of the origin of man as found in Genesis.

At the time the Supreme Court struck down the act, only two other states, Mississippi and Tennessee, had similar statutes.

In his concurring opinion, Justice Black raised the question as to whether the Court should have heard the case at all. He pointed out that the state had never enforced the law nor was there any indication that it intended to do so. He questioned if Miss Epperson were still teaching in the state or if the case had become moot. In effect, Black chided the state for its failure to provide up-to-date information about the case.

To Black, the case should have been decided entirely on the vagueness of the state statute. He added that he would not have invalidated the act on First Amendment establishment-of-religion grounds.

In their separate concurring opinions both Justices Harlan and Stewart would have struck down the statute for reasons of vagueness.

Free Exercise and Establishment

The First Amendment includes two concepts about religion: free exercise and establishment of religion. Cases heard by the Supreme Court have been decided by an interpretation of both clauses, although the establishment clause has been a decisive factor in a majority of the school cases.

The free exercise clause protects the individual in several respects. A basic right guaranteed by the clause allows persons to believe or to hold to any religious doctrine or dogma. Furthermore, free exercise grants an individual the right to follow his conscience and to worship in such manner as he believes his religion requires. An individual is free to exercise belief, disbelief, or non-belief. Laws may not curb one's beliefs or opinions, but they may collide with religious practices. A violation occurs when some form of coercion exists, such as compelling one to subscribe to a religious belief or to participate in a sectarian ceremony.

Although the free exercise clause allows a citizen to hold beliefs as his conscience dictates, it limits the extent to which one may practice his beliefs when the rights of others are infringed or harmed. This makes the law of the land superior to the individual's actions and prevents a citizen from becoming a law unto himself. The general rule is that one may practice a doctrine which is consistent with established morality and does not violate society's laws. The legality of a practice may not be so easy to decide as might appear at first blush. The problem results in balancing the individual's rights with the community's interests as expressed by the police power. When these two collide the courts are then called upon to resolve the conflict.

In the First Amendment there is included the second religion clause, the establishment clause. This one also protects the individual from government. It prohibits government from favoring one religion over another, many religions over some, or all religions over none. The federal government cannot establish a religion such as is found in England. In the meaning that the United States might set up an official church, the establishment of religion clause has not been seriously attacked under the Constitution.

Another purpose of the establishment clause is to protect the government from promoting one religious belief at the expense of another religion or even at the expense of non-believers. The term thus denotes a prohibition on laws which disfavor as well as favor religion. Moreover, a law compelling participation in a religious activity constitutes an establishment of religion. Thus, a person enjoys a right to be free from any government-sanctioned religion and to be free from any compulsion to support religion.

As interpreted by the Supreme Court, the establishment clause means that a "wall of separation" has been erected between church and state. Precedent for the use of this metaphor comes from Thomas Jefferson who, in writing to the Baptists at Danbury in 1802 said:

> Believing with you that religion is a matter which lies solely between man and his God, that he owes account to none other for his faith or his worship, that the legislative powers of government reach actions only, and not opinions, I contemplate with sovereign reverence that act of the whole American people which declared that their legislature should "make no law respecting an establishment of religion, or prohibiting the free exercise thereof," thus building a wall of separation between Church and State (49).

Although a rather complete separation of church and state has been insisted upon, some issues have not yet been settled. The United States, while not a religious nation, is primarily a country of religious people. The attitudes and traditions of Americans have prompted legislation which affected religions, religious institutions, and nondenominational schools. Separation has become a matter of degree rather than an absolute. Changes in the population structure and the religious beliefs of the American people have altered the application of the First Amendment. From over the world people have come to this country with various sectarian beliefs. They have settled in many localities, resulting in a heterogeneous religious population. When their children attend the local public schools, the religious stratification of the pupils reflects that of the community. Such a situation did not exist at the time of the adoption of the First Amendment. In arriving at decisions affecting religion in the schools, justices must be aware now of the growing public school system, the divergent religious population, and the sensitivity of the citizens within the school community. More specifically, a justice must examine the law as it affects the individual's religious conscience with the practices in the public schools.

The Supreme Court first defined the establishment clause in the dictum of Justice Black's opinion in *Everson* v. *Board of Education (50)*. This paragraph has since been referred to and relied upon in subsequent cases and has actually become more than dictum. Said Black:

> The "establishment of religion" clause of the First Amendment means at least this: Neither a state nor the Federal Government can set up a church. Neither can pass laws which aid one religion, aid all religions, or prefer one religion over another. Neither can force nor influence a

RELIGION

>person to go to or to remain away from church against his will or force him to profess a belief or disbelief in any religion. No person can be punished for entertaining or professing religious beliefs or disbeliefs, for church attendance or non-attendance. No tax in any amount, large or small, can be levied to support any religious activities or institutions, whatever they may be called, or whatever form they may adopt to teach or practice religion. Neither a state nor the Federal Government can, openly or secretly, participate in the affairs of any religious organizations or groups and vice versa. In the words of Jefferson, the clause against establishment of religion by law was intended to erect "a wall of separation between Church and State (51)."

In the prayer cases the Supreme Court's decision was based upon the establishment clause. In each case the Court was called upon to decide if the state had involved itself in the promotion of religion. Both *Engel* and *Schempp* (52) were similar to *McCollum* (53) in that in each situation the state permitted religious instruction in a public school. The activities were conducted during the school hours. Moreover, the school building was used for the religious activities. Each school system provided for student excusal from the exercises. When the Supreme Court heard the cases the justices decided in each instance that the establishment clause had been violated. Whereas the Court did not find a total establishment or the degree of support that government gave to religion in America's infancy, the justices felt that even a limited involvement infringed on the liberties of the people and thus could not be sustained.

In *Engel* Black discussed the establishment clause at length. At the outset he agreed with the petitioners that in the public schools the prayer's use—either required or permitted by the state—was a violation of the clause. He maintained that the prayer's use was unconstitutional in that government had composed it and the school, as an agency of the government, was promoting a religious belief through its recitation.

To substantiate his holding in *Engel*, Black relied on a study of history, going as far back as the adoption of the Book of Common Prayer by the established church of England. At the time of the authorization of the use of the book, people disagreed as to what should be included in it and how exercises should be conducted. These disagreements among other reasons, Black held, prompted settlers to come to America. He recognized, though, that, once here, some of the colonists set up established churches in their own right. Many of the people who were engaged in the Revolutionary War opposed an official religion. Black continued with his discussion of the clause:

>These people knew, some of them from bitter personal experience, that one of the greatest dangers to the freedom of the individual to worship in

his own way lay in the Government's placing its official stamp of approval upon one particular kind of prayer or one particular form of religious services. . . . The First Amendment was added to the Constitution as a guarantee that neither the power nor the prestige of the Federal Government would be used to control, support or influence the kinds of prayer the American people can say—that the people's religion must not be subjected to the pressures of government for change each time a new political administration is elected to office *(54).*

Justice Black held that, even though the Regents' Prayer was denominationally neutral, the establishment clause had been violated. The fact that students could voluntarily participate did not remove it from the zone of unconstitutionality. Black then differentiated between the establishment clause and the free exercise clause, saying:

The Establishment Clause, unlike the Free Exercise Clause, does not depend upon any showing of direct governmental compulsion and is violated by the enactment of laws which establish an official religion whether those laws operate directly to coerce nonobserving individuals or not. . . . When the power, prestige and financial support of government is placed behind a particular religious belief, the indirect coercive pressure upon religious minorities to conform to the prevailing officially approved religion is plain. But the purposes underlying the Establishment Clause go much further than that. Its first and most immediate purpose rested on the belief that a union of government and religion tends to destroy government and degrade religion *(55).*

In tracing further the historical significance of the establishment clause, Black indicated that persons with different religious beliefs expressed hatred and contempt when the English government or the colonies allied themselves with one religion. Religion is not successful when it has to rely upon government for its support, Black held. He concluded:

The Establishment Clause thus stands as an expression of principle on the part of the Founders of our Constitution that religion is too personal, too sacred, too holy, to permit its "unhallowed perversion" by a civil magistrate. Another purpose of the Establishment Clause rested upon an awareness of the historical fact that governmentally established religions and religious persecutions go hand in hand *(56).*

As if anticipating that persons might contend that the Supreme Court was being antireligious in this decision, Black had an answer. "The history of man is inseparable from the history of religion *(57),*" he said. He continued in showing the fact that men believed in the power of prayer as indicated by the people who left state-established religions in Europe and came to America where they could then pray as they wished. These persons with the same faith were those who wrote the Constitution and the Bill of Rights. "These men," Black wrote, "knew that the First Amendment which tried to put an end to governmental control of religion and of prayer, was not written to destroy either (58)." As Black saw the issue, rather than for government to direct men's speech through a type of prayer that is offered and to a God that one preferred, the Constitution, as interpreted through this decision, allows men to pray if and as they wish.

Black concluded his interpretation of the establishment clause by applying it to the New York prayer, saying:

> It is true that New York's establishment of its Regent's prayer as an officially approved religious doctrine of that State does not amount to a total establishment of one particular religious sect to the exclusion of all others—that, indeed, the governmental endorsement of that prayer seems relatively insignificant when compared to the governmental encroachments upon religion which were commonplace 200 years ago (59).

He then issued a warning which came from James Madison, "It is proper to take alarm at the first experiment on our liberties (60)."

Justice Douglas, in his concurring opinion, did not agree with the holding that the prayer amounted to an establishment of religion. To him, the problem was one of government's financing a religious activity. This will be considered later.

Justice Stewart's dissent took direct issue with the majority's interpretation of the establishment clause. Stewart maintained:

> With all respect, I think the Court has misapplied a great constitutional principle. I cannot see how an "official religion" is established by letting those who want to say a prayer say it. On the contrary, I think that to deny the wish of these children to join in reciting this prayer is to deny them the opportunity of sharing in the spiritual heritage of our Nation (61).

Stewart disagreed with Black's reliance on history for his reasoning. He did not accept Black's analogy of the established church in England with religion in this country. He noted that the states rejected an official church. Stewart further maintained that the history of an established church in England centuries ago was irrelevant; he held that the history of the religious traditions of the American people is the relevant issue.

Stewart's summary holding insisted:

> I do not believe that this Court, or the Congress, or the President has by the actions and practices I have mentioned established an "official religion" in violation of the Constitution. And I do not believe the State of New York has done so in this case. What each has done has been to recognize and to follow the deeply entrenched and highly cherished spiritual traditions of our Nation (62). . . .

In the *Schempp* case the justices also dealt with the establishment clause which, like *Engel*, decided the issue. In the majority opinion Justice Clark cited the eight religion cases affected by an establishment of religion that were decided by the Supreme Court, with only Justice Reed not agreeing that the clause prohibits the legislature from enacting laws affecting religious belief or an expression of that belief. Then Clark distinguished between the establishment clause and the free exercise clause:

> The wholesome "neutrality" of which this Court's cases speak thus stems from a recognition of the teachings of history that powerful sects or groups might bring about a fusion of governmental and religious functions or a concert or dependency of one upon the other to the end that official support of the State or Federal Government would be placed behind the tenets of one or of all orthodoxies. This the Establishment Clause prohibits. And a further reason for neutrality is found in the Free Exercise Clause, which recognizes the value of religious training, teaching and observance and, more particularly, the right of every person to freely choose his own course with reference thereto, free of any compulsion from the state. Thus the Free Exercise Clause guarantees *(63)*.

Clark concluded, in distinguishing the two clauses, that the element of coercion must be present in a case based upon free exercise while it does not have to be present in an establishment case. The justice found three factors in the Bible reading and prayer exercises which made them incompatible with the establishment clause: (1) The states required the selection and reading of the Bible and praying the Lord's Prayer at the opening of the school day. (2) The exercises were prescribed as part of the daily activities of the school which children are required by law to attend. (3) The exercises were held within the school under the teacher's supervision and with his participation.

Next, Clark recognized that the state admitted the religious nature of the exercises. He continued:

> The conclusion follows that in both cases the laws require religious exercises and such exercises are being conducted in direct violation of the rights of the appellees and petitioners *(64)*.

The rights of the majority were next treated by Clark. He had an answer for the contention that the majority could determine that the exercises could be held:

> Finally, we cannot accept that the concept of neutrality, which does not permit a State to require a religious exercise even with the consent of the majority of those affected, collides with the majority's right to free exercise *(65)*.

In his concurring opinion, Justice Douglas indicated that the estab-

RELIGION

lishment clause was violated on two counts: the state was conducting a religious exercise, and public funds were being spent to promote a religious activity. Douglas held that the first count violates the neutrality principle of the First Amendment, while the second cannot be sustained, since some people are required to contribute to a religious activity with which they are not in agreement.

Douglas then clarified his concept of the First Amendment. He wrote:

> While the Free Exercise Clause of the First Amendment is written in terms of what the State may not require of the individual, the Establishment Clause, serving the same goal of individual religious freedom, is written in different terms.
> Establishment of a religion can be achieved in several ways. The church and state can be one; the church may control the state or the state may control the church; or the relationship may take one of several possible forms of a working arrangement between the two bodies *(66)*.

Douglas pointed out that, in this country, schools were once under the supervision of the churches. He indicated that in some countries the public schools must still conduct religious exercises. He decried this, indicating that the church is using the state to gain supporters. He said:

> Under the First Amendment it is strictly a matter for the individual and his church as to what church he will belong to and how much support, in the way of belief, time, activity or money, he will give to it *(67)*....

Douglas concluded his opinion:

> For the First Amendment does not say that some forms of establishment are allowed; it says that "no law respecting an establishment of religion" shall be made. What may not be done directly may not be done indirectly lest the Establishment Clause become a mockery *(68)*.

Justice Brennan's lengthy concurring opinion treated historically the establishment clause. After reviewing past Supreme Court decisions, Brennan held that the clause "was designed comprehensively to prevent those official involvements of religion which would tend to foster or discourage religious worship or belief *(69)*."

While going back to the early history of this country, Brennan theorized that the framers of the Constitution did not give any thought about the matter of devotional exercises in public schools. He felt that relying upon the history of that time would be best served by consideration only of broad purposes rather than of details. Using such a guide, he held that the religious exercises in question were violations of the establishment clause. He indicated that there may be more serious violations of the First Amendment than was the Regents' Prayer, for the instruments used in the *Schempp* case are more sectarian.

Brennan gave no encouragement to those who maintained that the element of excusal should save the prayers' being allowed to be said. He answered:

> Thus the short, and to me sufficient, answer is that the availability of excusal or exemption simply has no relevance to the establishment question, if it is once found that these practices are essentially religious exercises designed at least in part to achieve religious aims through the use of public school facilities during the school day *(70)*.

Religion in Opening Exercises

Black indicated in *Engel* that there was no question about the religious aspect of the Regents' Prayer. He said about the prayer:

> It is a solemn avowal of divine faith and supplication for the blessings of the Almighty. The nature of such a prayer has always been religious, none of the respondents has denied this and the trial court expressly so found *(71)*: . . .

In *Schempp* Clark also pointed out that the devotional exercises were religious practices. He wrote:

> Applying the Establishment Clause principles to the cases at bar we find that the States are requiring the selection and reading at the opening of the school day of verses from the Holy Bible and the recitation of the Lord's Prayer by the students in unison. These exercises are prescribed as part of the curricular activities of students who are required by law to attend school. They are held in the school buildings under the supervision and with the participation of teachers employed in those schools. . . . The trial court . . . has found that such an opening exercise is a religious ceremony and was intended by the State to be so. We agree with the trial court's finding as to the religious character of the exercises *(72)*.

In addition to establishing the religious characteristics of the exercises, the justices showed that the practices preferred some religions over others. In *Schempp* Clark pointed out that the King James version of the Bible was generally used.

While both programs provided for voluntary participation, the teacher still led in the exercises. Although the New York prayer provided for the excusal of students, the actual machinery of operating the provision was often not put to use. A practical question concerned the desirability of students' leaving the room for the approximately fifteen seconds required to say the prayer. With the children in the room, the teacher directed the prayer exercises.

Slightly different circumstances occurred in *Schempp,* although the teacher's influence was still evident. Students read the Bible over the intercommunication system. After this was completed, the teacher issued a call for prayer whereby students were asked to stand and recite the Lord's Prayer in unison. If students were released from the room, they could still hear the Bible reading, as the sound from the public address system carried into the halls as well as in the classrooms. A student might have observed a less reverent attitude while not under the teacher's supervision, but the pupil was still within hearing range of the devotional exercises.

Teacher supervision amounted to teacher promotion of the exercises, and his guidance and leadership could not be minimized. He was at the front of the room—the focal point for the performance of the daily routine. The teacher thus aided in the implementation of the exercises. If he shared the conviction of the content of the Bible reading and prayers, he helped to foster that feeling. If he did not agree with the substance of the devotion, he still had to promote it, creating thereby an atmosphere of artificiality. Impressionable children were subject to being steered into the activity by the teacher who promoted the religious activities.

Standing to Sue

In *Engel* and *Schempp* the Supreme Court might have refused to have heard the appeals. The justices could have selected one of two alternatives, invoking the principle of *de minimis* or recognizing that the plaintiffs lacked standing to sue. The doctrine of *de minimis* holds that a problem is so insignificant or inconsequential as to preclude its being heard by the Court. To some critics of the decisions under study, this was the alternative the justices should have taken. Thus, the complaining parents might not have had recourse in the courts for lack of a substantial problem, no real injury having been shown.

The second alternative the Court might have taken would have been to refuse to hear the case while recognizing that the parties lacked standing. The plaintiffs showed no special injury as individuals and they claimed no financial loss. Their only basis for appeal to the High Court was to test the constitutionality of state action.

Standing was treated differently in *Allen.* There the Court did not consider standing to sue solely on the basis of a given question in dispute; rather, it treated the subject broadly. Moreover, there was not a specific litigious issue to be settled; instead, the Court was asked generally to allow suits involving specific constitutional questions. This plea was accepted by the justices who restricted the right to cover controversies surrounding the expenditure of funds conflicting with the establishment or free exercise clauses.

Where a plaintiff can show no harm different from the interest of the public in general, he is normally not accorded standing to sue. Where religious coercion exists, the problem can usually be easily satisfied. When the appellant can show that a practice affects his personal freedom to exercise his religion, he can base his claim on the free exercise clause of the First Amendment.

In the Bible-reading and prayer cases the action was predicated upon the establishment clause rather than upon the free exercise clause. The parents likely were more concerned about the effect of the practice upon their children and less concerned about an official establishment of religion. To gain standing before the Court, the plaintiffs had to show either that they had suffered a financial loss—different from that suffered by taxpayers in general—or that they had been subject to coercion in the practice of religion. In both cases the majority opinions relied upon the coercive element. In *Engel* Justice Black spoke of coercion as being indirect, for the state had used its "power, prestige and financial support." He did not indicate any financial loss to the complainants which was different from that of other taxpayers.

In *Schempp* Clark treated the doctrine of standing to sue in a footnote. He said:

> It goes without saying that the laws and practices involved here can be challenged only by persons having standing to complain. But the requirements for standing to challenge state action under the Establishment Clause, unlike those relating to the Free Exercise Clause, do not include proof that particular religious freedoms are infringed. . . . The parties here are school children and their parents, who are directly affected by the laws and practices against which their complaints are directed. These interests surely suffice to give the parties standing to complain *(73)*.

The opinion in *Schempp* indicated that there might be coercion merely from the existence of laws which advocated a particular devotional exercise. This position is no different from that taken by Black in *Engel*. Both decisions showed that state authority should not be exercised in putting pressure indirectly upon people to conform to a voluntary program.

Coercion in Religious Exercises

The element of coercion prompts two questions. Should children of minority religious groups elect not to participate and subject themselves to being singled out by other students and teachers as being non-conformists? Should these students participate in exercises contrary to what they believe and have been taught? First, there must be an understanding of the child in the public school. He is younger and less intellectually developed than is an adult; consequently, he is less likely to evaluate—or be able to evaluate—conflicting religious beliefs objectively. The child is more likely to be influenced in his thinking than is an adult. On the basis of that reasoning, the justices apparently framed their decision.

In New York the complaining parents objected to the use of the prayer, for they felt that its very use involved some coercion. This, they held, violated the establishment clause. Justice Black, answering in *Engel*, stated that the clause places an absolute prohibition on the state. He gave two reasons for this view. He indicated that whenever the state places its "power, prestige and financial support" behind a particular religious belief, it may place an "indirect coercive pressure upon religious minorities to conform *(74)*." The opinion also held that whenever government and religion unite, the result is a tendency to "destroy government and to degrade religion *(75)*."

The Schempp family were more adamant in their opposition to the religious exercises. They decided, for several reasons, not to have their children excused. The parents were concerned that their offspring might be labeled as being "odd balls." They feared that other students might brand their three children as being communistic or atheistic rather than tolerate them for holding a different religious belief. The elder Schempps also felt that placing the students in the hall was tantamount to being punished as offenders. Moreover, being in the hall would likely cause the children to miss the morning announcements which were made immediately after the students recited the Lord's Prayer and gave the flag salute.

The Court did not consider what possible effects the element of coercion might have upon the child's personality development. The sense of outward identification with the group and the feeling of inner security—components for a healthy education—were not treated directly by the justices in either case.

Once the Court granted *certiorari*, the justices felt obligated to deal with the question of Bible reading and prayer in full. To have done otherwise would have been to have delayed an ultimate answer; to have given a restricted decision would have been to affect only a limited number of school districts. The Court, for example, could have dealt only with the rights of the dissenting children. It could have upheld the prayer exercises while allowing an excusal privilege. To have done so, however, would have left unsolved the prayer exercises conducted in many school districts in which litigation might not arise. That, in effect, might have had the effect of sanctioning the exercises unless there were complaining parties. The justices could have given the impression that a public school might sponsor Bible reading and prayers if the community agreed and if there were no complaining parties. Brennan and Stewart recognized in their separate opinions that a parent could send his child to a private school and escape being exposed to an alien dogma. Stewart, though, met this issue by holding that most parents could not financially afford this.

Voluntary Participation

Both Black in *Engel* and Clark in *Schempp* recognized that participation in the exercises was voluntary. Both justices held, however, that this factor could not sustain their constitutionality. Black said:

> Neither the fact that the prayer may be denominationally neutral nor the fact that its observance on the part of students is voluntary can save to free it from the limitations of the Establishment Clause *(76)*. . . .

Clark cited and agreed with Black's holding. In *Schempp* he added that:

> Nor are these required exercises mitigated by the fact that individual students may absent themselves upon parental request, for that fact furnishes no defense to a claim of unconstitutionality under the Establishment Clause *(77)*.

To Black, voluntary participation was irrelevant; establishment was the key issue. The fact that students could abstain from participation inside the room or leave the room was not germane to the issue, for governmental compulsion is no part of a state's offense in a case affecting the establishment clause as it is in a free exercise case.

In sum, the Court held in the two cases that the recital of a prayer and the reading of selected Bible verses abridged the rights of individuals guaranteed by the First and the Fourteenth Amendments. Voluntary participation did not alter the legal question.

Rights of the Majority and Minority

Clark's opinion in *Schempp* revealed that the establishment clause serves as a check on legislative bodies concerning any action they may take affecting religious belief and the expression of that belief. The Court recognized the importance of worship when Clark's opinion pointed out that 64 per cent of the American people hold church memberships while only 3 per cent claim no religion *(78)*. Since a very small percentage of people claim no church ties, could not the Constitution uphold the majority's wishes in staging devotional exercises? Stated conversely, must a small segment of the school population deny the majority the right of worship for a few minutes each day? Clark rejected the notion that a majority could control such action. He said:

> While the Free Exercise Clause clearly prohibits the use of state action to deny the rights of free exercise to *anyone*, it has never meant that a majority could use the machinery of the State to practice its beliefs *(79)*.

Should the majority rule hold in such religious matters, the effect would be the establishment of a state church or of many state churches. It is conceivable that the religious majority in every state legislature could pass laws for the observance of religious exercises. In the absence of such state legislation it is even conceivable that local school districts could "establish" a form of religion through specified exercises. The Court has emphasized, therefore, that rule by majority is not in effect in matters of religion. Government may not prescribe religious exercises, for an individual may worship or refrain from worshiping as he wishes, or he may believe or not believe as he chooses.

The ruling of the Court thus is a victory for minority groups. While the decisions indicate no preference for any religion over another, they also show no favoritism to religion over no religion. That is to say, the 3 per cent who profess no religion have equal standing in the school room with the 64 per cent who hold church memberships. The First Amendment extends its constitutional protection to all. Were a majority of the people to try to force their beliefs or practices on people whose opinions are contrary to the minority, the result would be an establishment of religion. The Clark decision affirms that religious activity and state authority shall be kept separate.

Government Neutrality

The religious pluralism of the American people has created problems involving the relationship of government and religion. It is virtually impossible for a state to be involved in a religious activity which would be compatible with the beliefs of such divergent denominations. Clark pointed out in *Schempp* that there are now eighty-three sects in this country having over 50,000 members each *(80)*. In addition, there are many other sects with smaller memberships. Both *Engel* and *Schempp* recognized that, to avoid favoring a group, the state may not claim to promote a religious function within the framework of public education. Moreover, the state's purpose in education is not to make the pupils religious but to develop citizens who will assume responsibility for themselves and for the good of all. This objective prompts the state to offer to all children the opportunity for education through the public schools. This goal may be achieved while yet keeping the state neutral in matters of religion.

Since the state is neutral in religion, the public schools must also be neutral. In analyzing *Schempp*, Canavan states:

> The Court's intention was to make the state neutral in religion. It did not succeed, however, in making the state neutral in education. The separation of religion and education does not make schools religiously neutral. It only imposes a particular educational philosophy on the public schools, one that is most acceptable to people who consider religion irrelevant to life *(81)*.

Neutrality, through the Court's decisions, thus implies that the state respect all religious belief or unbelief. The schools teach from no ultimate religious point of view; they operate with a neutral perspective. Thus, the schools do not require that their students profess a religious belief; rather, they subscribe to the notion that all religious doctrines are of equal value.

Religious pluralism dictates also that, since the public schools are operated for all citizens, they must advocate no religious doctrine. Religion is too personal and too sacred to be left to government. Should there be only one faith among the citizens of a community, the neutrality principle still prohibits the school from espousing that religious view. At the same time, the school cannot promote a doctrine of anti-religion. This does not mean that schools are irreligious, as the Court noted in both *Engel* and *Schempp*. In *Schempp* the controlling opinion held that objective study of religion was permissible, although religious exercises in the public schools were impermissible. The neutrality principle, according to the Court, recognizes there is no distinction between the holding of religious exercises and the teaching of religion.

The treatment of the neutrality concept in *Engel* is not so thorough as that in *Schempp*. In *Engel* Black recognized, nonetheless, the government's incapacity to conduct religious exercises when he spoke:

When the power, prestige and financial support of government is placed behind a particular religious belief, the indirect coercive pressure upon religious minorities to conform to the prevailing officially approved religion is plain *(82)*.

Schempp advanced the doctrine more specifically by citing the principle of neutrality as being "wholesome." That decision indicated that the principle can be breached by government sponsorship of a religious exercise or by enactment of a law that advances or inhibits religion. In *Epperson*, Fortas recognized that the Arkansas law was not structured to promote religious neutrality.

The establishment clause thus stands as a safeguard to prevent the interference of government with religion. Since government can neither endorse nor exert its influence concerning a particular religious belief, the establishment clause bears a neutral command: government can neither favor nor disfavor any religious tenet. A violation of the command, as shown by Black, creates pressures for people to conform and results in subsequent hostility. The clause protects groups of people whose religious convictions are in the majority, those who hold minority views, as well as the non-believers. This is the Court's interpretation of neutrality as applied to establishment.

State Sponsorship and Endorsement

In looking at the immediate problem in *Engel*, the Supreme Court had a narrow constitutional question to decide, whether a prayer written and endorsed by the state could be sustained. The fact that the prayer was the product of the government made the decision easy to resolve. The majority opinion held that a governmental provision which required or permitted a prayer violated the establishment clause and, in doing so, produced some ideas about the relationship of church and state in American society. The Court indicated that government is powerless to prescribe any form of prayer to be used in government activity. The Court did not hold, however, that all prayer was barred from the public schools. It held that "it is no part of the business of government to compose official prayers for any group of the American people to recite as a part of a religious program carried on by the government *(83)*."

Black pointed out that persecutions and hatred go hand-in-hand with established religions. Were the state to sponsor a prayer, the activity might be changed each time new officials were elected to office.

In *Schempp* the Court expanded its holding. What the Court said through Clark was that the establishment clause prohibits state involvement in the holding of a religious activity. The public schools thus cannot constitutionally hold a religious exercise or promote a religious activity. The school must be a secular agency, for as the state has no religion, neither does the school.

Clark pointed out a danger of the state's becoming involved in religious activities. He indicated, as did Black, that religious groups could conceivably bring enough pressure upon government to force the government to favor one sect.

The facts differed in *Schempp* and in *Engel* in that the Lord's Prayer was not written by the state but was recommended by the state for use within the schools. The real issue was not the author but the sponsorship of the prayer. This caused both exercises to fall under the constitutional ban.

Sectarianism and Secularism

The establishment clause protects a statute enacted for a secular purpose and having a secular effect. Thus, the two factors are very important in weighing the constitutionality of religious measures. In both *Engel* and *Schempp* the Court found that both purpose and effect were primarily religious rather than secular, and thus it could not uphold them.

One of the problems lower courts have faced in handling religion cases affecting the public schools is their interpretation of sectarian education. The courts have not been in agreement about whether or not the Bible is sectarian. Justices holding that it is not sectarian have upheld religious instruction in the schools. This was the position taken by the defendants in *Schempp*. In their argument before the Pennsylvania federal court, the Abington School District was assisted by Dr. Luther A. Weigle, dean emeritus of the Yale Divinity School, who testified that the Bible and the Lord's Prayer were non-sectarian. However, in cross-examination, he qualified his position by conceding that the Bible and the Lord's Prayer were non-sectarian within the Christian faith.

In direct contrast with the above view is the belief that the Bible is sectarian. Adherents to this position contend that religion itself is sectarian and the use of the Bible incorporates sectarian belief. To offset Weigle's testimony, the Schempp family called on Dr. Solomon Grayzel, a Jewish expert who declared that the New Testament was unsuitable for Jewish children. He pointed out that portions of the New Testament were sectarian and were offensive to the Jewish people. He testified that such material could be presented to Jewish children with no harm, provided the material was explained. Of course, neither

Pennsylvania nor Maryland allowed this to be done. The mere reading of passages which might arouse controversy could therefore lead to sectarian strife.

Jewish literature does not contain the Lord's Prayer. Moreover, the prayer is not to be found in non-Christian religions. The Catholic and Protestant versions differ, and there are different versions among the Protestants. Some denominations entreat, "forgive us our debts, as we forgive our debtors," while others recite, "forgive us our trespasses as we forgive those who trespass against us." Also, some people have questioned if an all-wise God would lead people into temptation, as the next sentence of the prayer might imply. These differences of belief about and attitude toward the Lord's Prayer have their basis in sectarian reasons.

In both *Engel* and *Schempp* the Supreme Court held that the exercises smacked of sectarianism. The justices could not uphold the contention that the practices were acceptable to all faiths and preferential to none. Had they done otherwise, this would have been at variance with the Maryland action in which atheism, or the absence of religious faith, was the basis for the legal action.

Another point of departure is the assumption that all religions are based upon a belief in a personal God. There are exceptions to this, two being the Buddhist religion and Ethical Culture Society. A government which provides for a prayer acknowledging the existence of a personal God in actuality gives preferential treatment to some religions over others. Thus, the Regents' Prayer, "Almighty God, we acknowledge our dependence upon Thee," was found to be unconstitutional. The prayer was not the product, however, of any particular religious group; it had its origin in the state. It could be termed secular in origin but sectarian in content. The substance still acknowledged a Supreme Being, and the activity amounted to a religious exercise.

Financing Religious Exercises

In his concurring opinions in both *Engel* and *Schempp* Justice Douglas indicated that his primary concern was government financing of a religious exercise. He indicated at the outset that this was the pivotal point of the case in *Engel*. He continued by mentioning the ways in which government is currently aiding religion:

> There are many "aids" to religion in this country at all levels of government. To mention but a few at the federal level, one might begin by observing that the very First Congress which wrote the First Amendment provided for chaplains in both Houses and in the armed services.

There is compulsory chapel at the service academies, and religious services are held in the federal hospitals and prisons. The President issues religious proclamations. The Bible is used for the administration of oaths. N.Y.A. and W.P.A. funds were available to parochial schools during the depression. Veterans receiving money under the G.I. Bill of 1944 could attend denominational schools, to which payments were made directly by the government. During World War II, federal money was contributed to denominational schools for the training of nurses. The benefits of the National School Lunch Act are available to students in private as well as public schools. The Hospital Survey and Construction Act of 1946 specifically made money available to non-public hospitals. The slogan In God We Trust is used by the Treasury Department, and Congress recently added God to the pledge of allegiance. There is Bible-reading in the schools of the District of Columbia, and religious instruction is given in the District's National Training School for Boys. Religious organizations are exempt from the federal income tax and are granted postal privileges. Up to defined limits—15 per cent of the adjusted gross income of individuals and 5 per cent of the net income of corporations—contributions to religious organizations are deductible for federal income tax purposes. There are no limits to the deductibility of gifts and bequests to religious institutions made under the federal gift and estate tax laws. This list of federal aids could easily be expanded, and of course, there is a long list in each state *(84)*.

To Douglas, such aid is "an unconstitutional undertaking whatever form it takes *(85)*." He pointed out further in his opinion that the teacher who leads the prayer is on the payroll the same as chaplains for Congress and the Supreme Court Marshal. He indicated that, although the time the teacher spends in leading the exercises is very small, the principle is nonetheless the same. Further, Douglas indicated that a religion is not established by authorization of the use of the prayer. "Yet," he said, "once government finances a religious exercise it inserts a divisive influence into our communities *(86)*."

Later in the opinion Douglas referred to the *Everson* case and indicated a change of attitude. He had voted with the majority in that case which upheld a statute authorizing the reimbursement of parents for money spent in transporting their children to parochial schools. Douglas said:

My problem today would be uncomplicated but for *Everson* . . . which allowed taxpayers' money to be used to pay "the bus fares of parochial school pupils as a part of a general program under which" the fares of pupils attending public and other schools were also paid. The *Everson* case seems in retrospect to be out of line with the First Amendment. Its result is appealing, as it allows aid to be given to needy children. Yet by the same token, public funds could be used to satisfy other needs of children in parochial schools—lunches, books and tuition being obvious examples *(87)*.

In *Schempp* Douglas pointed out that the exercises were violated for two reasons: the state was conducting a religious exercise and public funds were being used to promote a religious activity. He held that the establishment clause:

> ... forbids the State to employ its facilities or funds in a way that gives any church, or all churches, greater strength in our society than it would have by relying on its members alone. Thus, the present regimes must fall under that clause for the additional reason that public funds, though small in amount, are being used to promote a religious exercise. Through the mechanism of the State, all of the people are being required to finance a religious exercise that only some of the people want and that violates the sensibilities of others.
> *The most effective way to establish any institution is to finance it; and this truth is reflected in the appeals by church groups for public funds to finance their religious schools (88).*

Douglas held that government could not finance a religious exercise even to a small degree, without violating the establishment clause. He pointed out that it is not the amount of public money involved; it is the use of the funds which is critical. The First Amendment dictates that no funds shall be spent either directly or indirectly, according to Douglas.

An extended examination of the financing of religious exercises in the public schools is beyond the scope of this study. The controlling opinions did not consider finance in these cases to be of major import; the concurring opinions of Douglas have no legal weight. The consideration of the issue here stems from his having raised the question and from the fact that government financial aid to religion is controversial and is being debated now. Justice Douglas's opinion reflects the thinking of only one man on the Court, but the topic which concerns him was reflected in the *Allen* and *Flast* decisions. It is expected that the Court will hear additional cases over financial aid to parochial schools.

Related Religious Activities

Some issues involving religion in the public schools have not reached the Supreme Court. Moreover, the Court has not given a clear definition of what religion is. The Court has not ruled that all religious observances in the schools are unconstitutional; it has stated what schools cannot do, but it has not indicated what schools can do. The line separating the permissible from the forbidden has not been made clear. As if to allay the fears of those who felt that all religion should be taken from the schools, the Supreme Court's dicta gave some guidelines and reassurances in both *Engel* and *Schempp* about the study of religion.

In *Engel* Justice Black used a footnote to clarify the Court's position. He said:

> There is of course nothing in the decision reached here that is inconsistent with the fact that school children and others are officially encouraged to express love for our country by reciting historical documents such as the Declaration of Independence which contain references to the Deity or by singing officially espoused anthems which include the composer's professions of faith in a Supreme Being, or with the fact that there are many manifestations in our public life of belief in God. Such patriotic or ceremonial occasions have no true resemblance to the unquestioned religious exercise that the State of New York has sponsored in this instance *(89)*.

Justice Clark wrote in *Schempp*:

> In addition, it might well be said that one's education is not complete without a study of comparative religion or the history of religion and its relationship to the advancement of civilization. It certainly may be said that the Bible is worthy of study for its literary and historic qualities. Nothing we have said here indicates that such study of the Bible or of religion, when presented objectively as part of a secular program of education, may not be effected consistent with the First Amendment *(90)*.

In his concurring opinion Justice Brennan also had some words about the use of the Bible in instruction:

> The holding of the Court today plainly does not foreclose teaching *about* the Holy Scriptures or about the differences between religious sects in classes in literature or history. Indeed, whether or not the Bible is involved, it would be impossible to teach meaningfully many subjects in the social sciences or the humanities without some mention of religion. To what extent, and at what points in the curriculum, religious materials should be cited are matters which the courts ought to entrust very largely to the experienced officials who superintend our Nation's public schools. They are experienced in such matters, and we are not. We should heed Mr. Justice Jackson's caveat that any attempt by this Court to announce curricular standards would be "to decree a uniform, rigid and, if we are consistent, an unchanging standard for countless school boards representing and serving highly localized groups which not only differ from each other but which themselves from time to time change attitudes *(91)*."

Goldberg's concurring opinion relied on the footnote in *Engel* quoted above, and which was repeated by Goldberg in *Schempp*.

From the guidelines of the justices to determine whether or not practices can be sustained in the public schools, consideration is given to the following activities and practices. In the light of the decisions, an attempt will be made to clarify their legal status.

Study of religious literature. Study about what people have done and what they have believed would be permissible. For example, describing what Martin Luther did in the early 1500's and showing a

RELIGION

cause-and-effect relationship with his crusade is necessary for an understanding of the Reformation. A discussion of the wisdom of his work would not be acceptable to some groups. Having books available for students to read is consistent with the Supreme Court ruling. It would be questionable whether or not a pupil could be required to read a religious classic which advocated a doctrine alien to his own.

Religious music. This should not be played nor sung as part of a devotional exercise. A school, however, could have recordings illustrative of the contributions that music has made to the arts and to civilization.

Religious pageants. If presented in a religious way, such performances could not be upheld. It would seemingly be difficult to stage a sectarian play without infringing upon an individual's beliefs. The real question here, however, is the wisdom of the school officials in allowing a performance. Can the school justifiably give the time required for such a production? Is the nature of the play itself typically representative of the curriculum? In other words, are there not other curricular areas which would better serve as learning and teaching situations than through a religious program? The problem here is yet one of substance and degree. A Thanksgiving program is both religious and patriotic. To escape the ban on a religious exercise, a Thanksgiving play might need to be rewritten to remove the religious references to a Deity and to the beliefs of a given denomination. Christmas, Easter, and Hanukkah programs should not be given, for they are almost entirely religious celebrations, although it is true that work and school holidays have resulted from them. To strip such programs of their religious substance and to deal only with the historical aspect would probably save the program constitutionally but leave it devoid of any real meaning. Such programs would be better left to non-school groups.

Baccalaureate services. Baccalaureate programs have their roots in the graduation programs of the universities during the Medieval Period. They have been used in this country for a number of years in both the colleges and universities and in the high schools. According to a study by Dierenfield:

> The traditional Baccalaureate service appears to be firmly entrenched as a part of high school graduation activities in the American school system. Throughout the nation 86.84 per cent of the public schools conduct such exercises. Only in the East where 68.13 per cent use it, does its widespread popularity seem in danger. The larger the town the less likelihood of Baccalaureate activities being found. The answers to contingent questions point out some interesting practices. Nearly all schools which have these services hold them on school property and not in churches (85.63 per cent). Approximately two-thirds of the system (67.43 per cent) make Baccalaureate a voluntary affair *(92).*

Many baccalaureate programs include a visiting minister who delivers the address and one or more preachers who assist in the service such as by reading the scripture and praying. In addition to the sermon, the scripture, and the prayer, sacred music is often sung. Some of the programs are held within the school while others are conducted in local churches. There is no question but that the exercises held within the school are in violation of the Court's decree in *Engel* and *Schempp*. To make attendance voluntary would still be an abridgment of the Court's holding. A school might continue to hold the service in a church and make attendance voluntary. However, to ascertain whether this activity could be sustained is not so easily answered. It is recognized that the school is involved in the program through planning and participation. It is conceivable that the Court would overrule the exercise on the grounds that changing the locale of the program does not change the substance of it. Another position that might be taken is that the voluntary attendance and participation exerts, nonetheless, an indirect coercion to attend.

Chapel exercises. In some schools regular programs are given, sometimes as often as once a week, for the entire student body. The programs are conducted by pupils and teachers within the school as well as by persons, including ministers outside the school. Programs might include the singing of sacred music, reading of the scripture, prayer, and an inspirational message. The programs, designed almost entirely for a secular purpose, clearly violate *Engel* and *Schempp*.

Assembly programs. An assembly program differs from a chapel program in that the purpose of the former is secular; the latter, religious. Like the chapel program, an assembly may include all the pupils in the school. Some assemblies open with a devotional exercise such as reading of the scripture and a prayer. After this ritual, the program may then be entirely secular. The opening religious exercise would defy *Engel* and *Schempp*, for the school has merely taken the exercises condemned in the two cases from the classroom and transferred them to the auditorium. Removing the devotional aspects of the assembly program would not entail the curtailment of the other components of the school assembly.

May a school allow a minister to speak in an assembly program? Does the minister, as a representative of a given church or denomination, create an atmosphere of religion, and does his talk constitute an establishment of religion? Do *Engel* and *Schempp* forbid the appearance of a minister in a school program? A yes-or-no response does not answer the question. First, a minister could speak on a secular as well as on a religious topic. He could not constitutionally deliver a sermon, read from the scriptures, or pray. The content of his speech must necessarily avoid religious connotations. On the other hand, a minister could talk about a wide variety of topics and not offend the holding of either *Engel* or *Schempp*.

A second problem relates to a minister's dress in an assembly program. If he were clothed in distinctive religious garb, he would probably be transgressing the religious prohibition. Some lower courts have held that the wearing of clothes peculiar to a denomination constitutes an influence of religion. In order for a minister to be allowed to speak, he must therefore refrain from espousing a religious faith, from using devotional aids, and from wearing sectarian clothes.

Patriotic exercises. Questions have arisen following the *Engel* and *Schempp* decisions about the use of songs with references to God. Other problems relate to the study of historical documents such as the Declaration of Independence and to the recitation of the Pledge of Allegiance. Among the songs questioned are the national anthem and "America," both of which contain references to God. In the fourth verse of "The Star Spangled Banner" are these lines:

> Then conquer we must, when our cause it is just,
> And this be our motto—"In God is our Trust,"

The fourth verse of "America" states:

> Our fathers' God! to Thee,
> Author of liberty,
>   To Thee we sing;
> Long may our land be bright
> With freedom's holy light;
> Protect us by Thy might,
>   Great God, our King!

Along with the songs invoking a Deity is the pledge of allegiance to the flag which also makes a reference to God:

> I pledge allegiance to the flag of the United States of America and to the republic for which it stands. One nation, under God, indivisible, with liberty and justice for all.

The Declaration of Independence has four specific references to the Deity, two appearing at the beginning, two being at the end of the document:

> ... the separate and equal station to which the Laws of Nature and of Nature's God entitle them, ...

> . . . that they are endowed by their Creator with certain unalienable rights, . . .
>
> . . . appealing to the Supreme Judge of the world for the rectitude of our intentions . . .
>
> And for the support of this Declaration, with a firm reliance on the protection of divine Providence, . . .

Many school children are called upon to recite Lincoln's Gettysburg Address which states, in part:

> . . . that this nation, under God, shall have a new birth of freedom, . . .

The guides about the use of these activities are fairly clear from Black's footnote in *Engel*. Rather than to consider these activities to be religious, they are patriotic. The references to God in the national anthem and in "America" are the personal views of the composer, Black has said. Thus, singing such songs is a patriotic rather than a religious exercise. Likewise, a recitation from the Declaration of Independence and other historical documents and speeches is a patriotic exercise.

In *Schempp*, Goldberg, in his concurring opinion, quoted from Black's footnote and indicated that patriotic exercises should not be curtailed.

Religious holidays. Many schools include in their year's calendar of activities provision for the observance and celebration of religious holidays. Among the more commonly commemorated holidays are Easter, Thanksgiving, and Christmas. In observance of these occasions some schools present programs, and many schools do not hold session.

A school program in commemoration of a religious holiday is violative of *Engel* and *Schempp*. The reason for the program is religious, and the substance is necessarily religious also. This places the program behind the "power, prestige and financial support of government" which Black condemned in *Engel*. It also violates Clark's test of "purpose and primary effect" in *Schempp*.

In conjunction with religious holidays, two problems arise. One is the closing of school for a religious event; the other is releasing children from school to attend or to participate in the celebration during school time but away from school. Neither *Engel* nor *Schempp* offers a suggestion about the legality of either. *Zorach (93)* comes nearer to answering the second question. Justice Douglas held in that case that excusing students to attend religious classes during school time was a matter of cooperation between schools and the churches. The distinction in *Zorach* and in this situation is that the former involved religious curricular classes; the latter's concern is for an occasional absence from school for religious activities.

Displays. Usually schools have space and equipment within their classrooms for displays. Bulletin boards are found on the walls of most school rooms. A question arises as to whether the school room can be used for purposes such as a display of religious scenes, the Ten Commandments, pictures of religious leaders, the cross, or a miniature village of Palestine. Could a mural be displayed if it had a religious message? If the purpose of the displays was to have a primary religious effect, their being in the classroom would be prohibitive. If, however, they were used as teaching devices in conjunction with the study of history, they could be sustained. The real answer would likely turn on the specific situation. For example, a bulletin-board display showing a statement such as "God so loved the world that He gave His only begotten Son . . ." might be offensive to people for several reasons. First, it is using a portion of a verse of scripture which could bring objections from non-believers. Second, it is relying upon a given version of the Bible which could offend some denominations. Another objection might stem from the message of the verse itself. On the other hand, a bulletin board showing life in Palestine at the time of the birth of Christ could legitimately be presented without any religious connotations.

Use of the cross as a display would not likely be upheld, for the cross itself has its foundations in religion. Its being in the room would serve as a reminder, however subtle, of an establishment rather than of a historical relic.

Pictures of religious leaders might be shown in teaching the contributions of such people to history. The display of the Ten Commandments could not be sustained, for their source is in the Bible. The Commandments carry with them messages for people to follow. Some parents might object to the content of these commandments as having a divisive influence on their children.

In sum, the staging of displays in a classroom is not, within itself, in violation of *Engel* and *Schempp*. The legality turns on the purpose of the display. If the purpose is non-religious, then it can be upheld. The distinction between sectarian and secular may be fine, but it can be maintained.

The Bible in teaching. The Supreme Court has not said that the Bible and its use must be completely removed from the school. The justices have held, however, that the use of the Bible as a devotional exercise is prohibited by the First Amendment. May, then, the Bible be used in other aspects of instruction? Yes, if the purpose is non-sectarian and non-religious. It may be used to indicate what people have believed, not what one should believe. The former is a study of history; the latter is an imposition of a belief upon another. One may teach about the characteristics of the major faiths without asserting that one faith is correct or preferred to others.

For purposes of testing students, the same standard should prevail. Thus, a teacher should not tell students: "Christ was the Son of God." Not all religious groups subscribe to this idea, and the statement is without qualification.

Other curriculum controversies. Outside the social studies in which there is probably more controversy about religiously-oriented material, there are other issues discussed in the classroom to which people have objected as being counter to their views. A health class in which the teacher discusses the various uses of medication for purposes of healing stands to offend the Christian Scientists. Some denominations refute the idea that the earth is millions or billions of years old, and the teachers who teach this as fact incur disbelief from some students. Other issues of controversy deal with reproduction and birth control. Guidelines for teaching or not teaching these are not covered by *Engel* and *Schempp,* although Douglas did refer to the problem in *Allen.* Whether the Supreme Court would consider that the handling of such material constitutes an establishment of religion cannot be answered.

In attempting to clarify the role of the public schools with respect to teaching about religion. Johnson states that:

> ... the role of the American public school would likely seem to be limited to making known and understood the role which religion, as empirical fact, plays in the culture itself and in human history. To expect less of our schools is to take too narrow a view of general education; to demand more is to confuse the function of the school with that of home or church *(94).*

Hunt indicates that conferences have assigned the school the teaching of:

– ethical behavior based on a sense of moral and spiritual values;
– respect and appreciation for human values and for the beliefs of others;
– appreciation for our democratic heritage;
– civic rights and civic responsibilities;
– awareness of our relationship with the world community *(95).*

Summary

While not deciding what religion is, the Supreme Court has limited

RELIGION

religious exercises in the schools. With only Justice Stewart in the minority, the justices have agreed that state action which requires or permits the daily recitation of prayers and reading from the Holy Bible violates the establishment clause of the First Amendment. The Court has left unsettled many other religious questions involving the schools. A brief summary of the decisions follows.

Engel v. *Vitale (1962).* A state may not prescribe the use of a prayer within the schools. Action by the State Board of Regents of New York in providing for the use of a prayer exceeded the constitutionality of the establishment clause.

School District of Abington Township v. *Schempp* and *Murray* v. *Curlett (1963).* When a state requires the reading of scripture and the Lord's Prayer as daily devotional exercises, it violates the establishment clause of the First Amendment. The Supreme Court ruled from two separate but similar cases. In Pennsylvania a statute required the reading of ten verses of Scripture without comment. Baltimore required either the reading of Scripture or the use of the Lord's Prayer.

Chamberlin v. *Dade County (1964).* Relying upon *Schempp*, the Supreme Court held that a Florida statute which required the reading of Bible verses and recitation of the Lord's Prayer was unconstitutional. The Court did not act on the legality of other questionable religious activities in the Florida schools.

Board of Education v. *Allen (1968).* Law of New York State authorizing lending of textbooks to students in parochial schools is not an abridgment of the First Amendment.

Flast v. *Cohen (1968).* Individuals may bring suit against the government for expenditure of federal funds based on an alleged violation of separation of church and state.

Epperson v. *Arkansas (1968).* Arkansas law prohibiting the teaching of evolution in public schools and universities is in violation of the First Amendment.

In addition to the basic holdings of these cases, the Supreme Court has given some pertinent principles with respect to church-state relationships. To meet the test of constitutionality, legislative enactments providing for religion in education must have a secular purpose and a primary effect that does not promote nor stifle religion. Any legislation providing, in the main, for a religious exercise, does not meet the test of constitutionality under the establishment clause.

The role of the state in a religious exercise in the public schools is a neutral one. The state does not favor one religion nor all religions over none. That is to say, in a classroom an unbeliever has equal standing with a believer. The school may not promote a religious belief or an exercise which favors or disfavors any sectarian group. It matters not whether a school community is made up of a homogeneous religious population; what matters is state involvement.

Religious exercises providing for voluntary participation of pupils have no more constitutional standing than those without an excusal provision. Once the state promotes an activity, there is some degree of coercion for all to participate.

The Court has not stated that all religion shall be removed from the schools. It has not given precise limits as to what may or may not be done. The school must be committed to a principle of neutrality as it concerns religion; moreover, any study of religion must be objective. Beyond these guides, the Court opinions leave the matter to school officials, who will decide, in more specific situations, whether or not activities will be held.

Notes to Chapter III

1. *Cochran* v. *Louisiana State Board of Education*, 281 U.S. 370 (1930).
2. *Cantwell* v. *Connecticut*, 310 U.S. 296 (1940).
3. *Everson* v. *Board of Education of Ewing Township*, 330 U.S. 1 (1947).
4. *Engel* v. *Vitale*, 370 U.S. 421 (1962).
5. From "The Regents Statement on Moral and Spiritual Training in the Schools," *The University of the State of New York Bulletin to the Schools*, XXXVIII (December, 1951), 94.
6. *Engel, op. cit.*, p. 430.
7. *Ibid.*, p. 425.
8. *Ibid.*, p. 433.
9. *Ibid.*, p. 435.
10. *Ibid.*, p. 441.
11. *Ibid.*, p. 445.
12. *School District of Abington Township, Pennsylvania, et al.* v. *Schempp et al.*, 374 U.S. 203 (1963).
13. Richard B. Dierenfield, *Religion in American Public Schools* (Washington: Public Affairs Press, 1962), p. 50.
14. *Murray et al.* v. *Curlett et al., Constituting the Board of School Commissioners of Baltimore City*, 179 A. 2d (1962).
15. At the time of the *Schempp* decision, state courts had upheld Bible reading in the following states: Colorado, Georgia, Iowa, Kansas, Maine, Michigan, Nebraska, Ohio, and Texas. The following state courts had held Bible reading to be unconstitutional: Illinois, New Jersey, South Dakota, Washington, and Wisconsin.
16. *Murray, loc. cit.*
17. *Schempp, op. cit.*, p. 215.
18. *Ibid.*, p. 222.
19. *Ibid.*, p. 224.
20. *Ibid.*, p. 225.
21. *Ibid.*

RELIGION

22. *Ibid.*
23. *Ibid.*, p. 229.
24. *Ibid.*, p. 230.
25. *Ibid.*, p. 267.
26. *Ibid.*, p. 306.
27. *Ibid.*, p. 313.
28. *Murray, op. cit.*, p. 316.
29. *Chamberlin et al. v. Dade County Board of Public Instruction et al.*, 377 U.S. 402 (1964).
30. *Florida Statutes Annotated*, Section 231.09.
31. *Chamberlin v. Dade County Board of Public Instruction*, 143 So. 2d 21 (1962).
32. *Chamberlin*, 374 U.S. 487 (1963).
33. *Stein et al. v. Oshinsky, Principal, Public School 184, Whitestone, New York, et al.*, 382 U.S. 957 (1965).
34. *Board of Education of Central School District No. 1 et al. v. Allen, Commissioner of Education of New York, et al.*, 392 U.S. 236 (1968).
35. *Ibid.*, p. 247.
36. *Ibid.*, p. 271.
37. *Ibid.*, p. 250.
38. *Ibid.*, p. 252.
39. *Ibid.*, p. 253.
40. *Ibid.*, p. 257.
41. *Flast et al. v. Cohen, Secretary of Health, Education, and Welfare, et al.*, 392 U.S. 83 (1968).
42. *Frothingham v. Mellon*, 262 U.S. 447 (1923).
43. *Flast, op. cit.*, p. 99.
44. *Ibid.*, p. 102.
45. *Epperson et al. v. State of Arkansas*, 393 U.S. 97 (1968).
46. *Ibid.*, p. 103.
47. *Ibid.*, p. 106.
48. *Ibid.*, p. 107.
49. From a letter to Messrs. Nehemiah Dodge, Ephriam Robbins, and Stephen S. Nelson, A Committee of the Danbury Baptist Association, in the State of Connecticut, on January 1, 1802. The letter is taken from Saul K. Padover, *The Complete Jefferson: Containing His Major Writings, Published and Unpublished, Except His Letters* (New York: Duell, Sloan and Pearce, Inc., 1943), p. 518.
50. *Everson, loc. cit.*
51. *Ibid.*, p. 15.
52. Hereinafter, reference to *Schempp*, other than in direct quotations, will be used to denote both *Schempp* and *Chamberlin*, as the latter case was decided, based upon the holding of the former.
53. *Illinois ex rel. McCollum v. Board of Education of School District No. 71, Champaign County, Illinois et al.*, 333 U.S. 203 (1948).
54. *Engel, op. cit.*, p. 429.
55. *Ibid.*, p. 430.
56. *Ibid.*, p. 431.
57. *Ibid.*, p. 434.
58. *Ibid.*, p. 435.
59. *Ibid.*, p. 436.
60. *Ibid.*
61. *Ibid.*, p. 445.

62. *Ibid.*, p. 450.
63. *Schempp, op. cit.*, p. 222.
64. *Ibid.*, p. 224.
65. *Ibid.*, p. 226.
66. *Ibid.*, p. 227.
67. *Ibid.*, p. 228.
68. *Ibid.*, p. 230.
69. *Ibid.*, p. 234.
70. *Schempp, op. cit.*, p. 288.
71. *Engel, op. cit.*, p. 424.
72. *Schempp, op. cit.*, p. 223.
73. *Ibid.*, p. 224.
74. *Engel, op. cit.*, p. 431.
75. *Ibid.*
76. *Ibid.*, p. 430.
77. *Schempp, op. cit.*, p. 224.
78. *Ibid.*, p. 213.
79. *Ibid.*, p. 226.
80. *Ibid.*, p. 214.
81. Francis Canavan, "Implications of the School Prayer and Bible Reading Decisions: The Welfare State," *Journal of Public Law*, XIII (1964), 440.
82. *Engel, op. cit.*, p. 431.
83. *Ibid.*, p. 425.
84. *Ibid.*, p. 437. Douglas quotes directly from David Fellman, *The Limits of Freedom* (New Brunswick, New Jersey: Rutgers University Press, 1959), p. 41.
85. *Ibid.*
86. *Ibid.*, p. 442.
87. *Ibid.*, p. 443.
88. *Schempp, op. cit.*, p. 229.
89. *Engel, op. cit.*, p. 435.
90. *Schempp, op. cit.*, p. 225.
91. *Ibid.*, p. 300.
92. Dierenfield, *op. cit.*, p. 62.
93. *Zorach v. Clauson*, 343 U.S. 306 (1952).
94. F. Ernest Johnson, "A Problem of Culture," *Religion and the Schools* (New York: The Fund for the Republic, 1959), p. 66.
95. R. L. Hunt, "How Schools Can Teach Religious Values—Legally," *The Nation's Schools*, LXXIII (February, 1964), p. 49.

Chapter IV

SEGREGATION

Introduction

The Fourteenth Amendment makes no mention of schools or of education. Both, however, are subject to Section I of the Amendment which states:

> All persons born or naturalized in the United States and subject to the jurisdiction thereof, are citizens of the United States and of the State wherein they reside. No State shall make or enforce any law which shall abridge the privileges or immunities of citizens of the United States; nor shall any State deprive any person of life, liberty, or property, without due process of law; nor deny to any person within its jurisdiction the equal protection of the laws.

The clauses, "privileges or immunities," "due process," and "equal protection," have been the subject of much litigation, particularly with respect to segregation of the races in general and with separation of whites and Negroes in public schools in particular. After the Civil War and the adoption of the Fourteenth Amendment in 1868, some dual school systems were set up for the two races. Although Negroes received the same education in kind as whites, the quality and the quantity of their schooling were usually inferior.

Since the adoption of the Amendment and the formation of separate schools, legal problems have arisen concerning the application of the Amendment to the schools. Questions before the courts have concerned primarily the legality of differential treatment of the races. The "equal protection" clause has been the major source on which litigation has been predicated.

Segregation in the schools has undergone three legal phases: that resulting from the *Plessy* decision of 1896, the higher education cases beginning in the 1930's, and the public school cases beginning with the *Brown* decision of 1954. Although *Plessy* v. *Ferguson* dealt with segregation in transportation facilities rather than with schools, the Supreme Court's ruling was interpreted to be applicable to them. The decision resulted in a strict adherence by many states to the "separate but equal" doctrine. Justice Brown who wrote the majority opinion spoke of school segregation in the dicta. He said:

> The most common instance of this [laws requiring separation of the races] is connected with the establishment of separate schools for white and colored children, which has been held to be a valid exercise of the legislative power even by courts of States where the political rights of the colored race have been longest and most earnestly enforced (1).

The justice stated further that:

> The distinction between laws interfering with the political equality of the negro and those requiring the separation of the two races in schools, theatres and railway carriages has been frequently drawn by this court (2).

Although the "separate but equal" doctrine embraced by *Plessy* was generally followed in many states, only two cases were heard by the Supreme Court in the next fifty years which contested racial segregation in the public schools. Neither case directly challenged that doctrine.

The second legal phase grew out of an increase in population in the public schools and a corresponding increase in college enrollment. Attorneys for Negro students felt the time to be appropriate to challenge the separation principle. Accordingly, their legal strategy was carefully devised to make an initial attack on the graduate schools rather than the elementary and secondary schools. They reasoned that less unfavorable public reaction might result; moreover, they felt that winning their case would be better assured at the graduate level. If they were successful, they then felt that inroads could be made on the lower grades practicing segregation.

Phase two began with a case involving a Negro seeking admission to the School of Law at the University of Missouri (3). The state had no law school for Negroes, but it paid tuition for them to enroll in out-of-state institutions. In 1938 the Supreme Court of the United States held that this arrangement placed the petitioner at a disadvantage. The justices saw that advantages accrued in attending a law school in a state where one expected to practice. They ordered the student's admission to the School of Law.

Ten years later the Court struck down an Oklahoma law which denied Negroes admission to the University of Oklahoma Law School (4). Since the state made no provision for a law school for Negroes to attend, either in the state or outside it, the Court ordered the admission of Sipuel to the law school. Furthermore, the immediate relief requested was granted.

Following the *Sipuel* decision, the Court heard two years later a case also involving the University of Oklahoma. In *McLaurin* v. *Oklahoma State Regents* (5) the Court was asked to rule on the validity of forced segregation within the University. McLaurin, a Negro graduate student enrolled at the University, was assigned to designated seats in classrooms, the library, and the cafeteria—each place segregating him from white students. The Court struck down the restrictions, saying:

> There is a vast difference—a Constitutional difference—between restrictions imposed by the state which prohibit the intellectual commingling of students, and the refusal of individuals to commingle where the state presents no such bar *(6)*.

The justices recognized that the segregation to which McLaurin had been subjected restricted his ability to study, to engage in discussions with fellow students, and to exchange ideas necessary for one to learn.

On the same day that *McLaurin* was decided, the Supreme Court held that Herman Sweatt was entitled to be enrolled at the University of Texas Law School *(7)*. Unlike Missouri, Texas had a law school for Negroes. The Court, however, found an inequality in the two schools with respect to the size of the faculty, the number of volumes in the library, and the physical plant. The Court also recognized that it is a nonsegregated society in which lawyers circulate while engaged in their work.

By 1950 or near the end of the second legal phase of segregation, the Supreme Court had examined closely the "separate but equal" doctrine. It not only held to that principle but also sought to determine if segregated schools were, in fact, equal. A similar situation existed in the lower courts wherein the justices weighed comparable factors by which schools are judged, including among other things, building, finance, curriculum, and personnel. The *Plessy* doctrine was still operative, but its application was subject to closer scrutiny by the courts.

In the meantime, segregation had been ended by the 1953 school term in all schools operated by the Defense Department for children of military personnel. This included such southern states as Georgia, Kentucky, North Carolina, South Carolina, and Virginia *(8)*.

The end of the second legal phase marked an adherence to the "separate but equal" doctrine. The justices had been asked to repudiate the doctrine in *Sweatt* but had refused to do so. The four cases indicate that the justices exercised restraint in the decisions, for no action was taken beyond the issues involved in the specific cases. The justices had given no indication as to how they might react when faced with segregation in the public schools. One could speculate that the Court might recognize sufficient differences in public school education and in graduate schools to sustain the *Plessy* doctrine, or it could mean that, once the Court received a public school case, no differences could be discerned. However, the success of the attorneys in the graduate school cases prompted an attack on the segregated public school system. When the first *Brown* case came before the Court, the justices were confronted directly with the doctrine.

In cases before the Warren Court affecting the public schools, the justices had to deal first with segregation. To be sure, the first *Brown* case was initially argued in the Supreme Court before Earl Warren became Chief Justice. It was this case that began the third legal phase, the Court decisions deciding the legality of public school segregation. It also is the beginning of this chapter which starts with the initial attack on the "separate but equal" doctrine and reaches the climactic May 17, 1954, *Brown* decision. Within the chapter is presented a study of the original *Brown* cases, the implementation decision, and subsequent cases involving standards of desegregation.

The Cases

The segregation decision which outlawed racial classifications by public schools in the United States is commonly referred to as *Brown* v. *Board of Education (9)*. Actually, the decision involved four cases which arose in four different states: Kansas, South Carolina, Virginia, and Delaware. After the United States Supreme Court accepted the separate cases on appeal, it then joined them for the 1954 decision. The cases were initially appealed to the Court in 1952 *(10)* and oral arguments were requested the same year *(11)*. A year later the Court announced that no judgment had been reached *(12)*.

Case 1: *Brown* v. *Board (1954).* In *Brown et al.* v. *Board of Education of Topeka et al. (13),* the case arose under a Kansas statute permitting cities of first class (over 15,000) to maintain separate schools for whites and Negroes in grades one through eight. Under the law Topeka had separate schools for pupils enrolled in the first six grades.

The law was attacked in 1951 when Linda Brown, a Negro elementary pupil living five blocks from a white school, had to travel over four times that distance to a Negro school. The pupil's parents sought to enjoin the enforcement of Kansas law and the segregated school system and to declare the state law unconstitutional. They contended that segregation in and of itself causes inferiority and is thus a denial of due process and equal protection.

The United States District Court found that segregation in public education has a detrimental effect on Negro children. It declined to end segregation, however, when it found that the Kansas schools in question were substantially equal in facilities. It felt bound by previous United States Supreme Court decisions and held that absolute equality was impossible.

In September, 1953, the Topeka Board of Education voted to abolish elementary school segregation. It decided to end segregation as soon as possible under the Kansas local option clause.

Case 2: Briggs v. Elliott (1954). A second case, *Briggs v. Elliott (14)* grew out of South Carolina where parents attacked public school segregation in both the elementary and the high schools in Clarendon County. Separate schools for the races were maintained through both constitutional and statutory provisions.

As was done in Kansas, the National Association for the Advancement of Colored People assisted in the litigation, initially begun in 1950. The Eastern District Court of South Carolina found that Negro schools were inferior to the white schools and ordered that equal facilities be provided for the colored children. The Court sustained the validity of state laws requiring segregation. School officials were directed to report back to the Court within six months. The case was then immediately appealed to the United States Supreme Court.

Case 3: Davis v. School Board (1954). In Virginia Negro parents challenged segregation in *Davis v. County School Board of Prince Edward County (15).* Separate schools were maintained under both constitutional and statutory provisions. The United States District Court found that the Negro schools were inferior and ordered that equal facilities be provided. It directed that the Negro high school in Prince Edward County be replaced with a new building and equipment and that inequalities otherwise be removed. The plaintiffs then asked the Supreme Court to overrule the lower court and order children admitted to the white high school.

Case 4: Gebhart v. Belton (1954). The fourth of the cases, *Gebhart v. Belton (16),* arose in Delaware where the state constitutional and statutory provisions enforced public school segregation. A lower court decision held that segregation has a detrimental effect on Negro children and ordered that Negroes be immediately admitted to the public schools until such time as the Negro schools were made equal to those of the whites. The Delaware Supreme Court upheld the decision which did not treat segregation as such. The decision differed from those rendered in South Carolina and Virginia in that it stated the right of the plaintiffs to equal facilities to be present and personal. It held that schools could be separate if currently equal. School authorities appealed the decision, alleging that the state had not allowed a reasonable time for equalization.

The four states in question were not the only ones to sanction segregation of public schools. The following seventeen states required segregation by state constitutional or statutory law prior to 1954: Alabama, Arkansas, Delaware, Florida, Georgia, Kentucky, Louisiana, Maryland, Mississippi, Missouri, North Carolina, Oklahoma, South Carolina, Tennessee, Texas, Virginia, and West Virginia. Segregation was allowed under permissive legislation in Arizona, Kansas, New Mexico, and Wyoming *(17)*.

In the reargument before the Supreme Court, counsel were asked to present their views on the following:

> 1. What evidence is there that the Congress which submitted and the State legislatures and conventions which ratified the Fourteenth Amendment contemplated or did not contemplate, understood or did not understand, that it would abolish segregation in public schools?
> 2. If neither the Congress in submitting nor the States in ratifying the Fourteenth Amendment understood that compliance with it would require the immediate abolition of segregation in public schools, was it nevertheless the understanding of the framers of the Amendment
>   (a) that future Congresses might, in the exercise of their power under section 5 of the Amendment, abolish such segregation, or
>   (b) that it would be within the judicial power, in light of future conditions, to construe the Amendment as abolishing such segregation of its own force?
> 3. On the assumption that the answers to questions 2 (a) and (b) do not dispose of the issue, is it within the judicial power, in construing the Amendment, to abolish segregation in public schools *(18)*?

Several alternatives faced the Supreme Court. The justices could have continued the "separate but equal" doctrine. They could have reversed *Plessy* v. *Ferguson* based on a study of the historical intention of the Fourteenth Amendment. They could have reversed *Plessy* on the grounds that the Fourteenth Amendment prohibits all state action of an unreasonable discriminatory nature. Another alternative would have been a simple finding that the schools were equal. They could have found that sufficient distinctions between elementary and secondary school pupils and university students exist and refused to act. The Court, however, did none of these.

Chief Justice Warren stated that the history and purposes of the Fourteenth Amendment as it relates to education were "inconclusive." The Court could not determine what the Amendment's framers had in mind relative to education. Moreover, as Warren indicated, public education was not fully developed at the time of the Amendment's adoption in 1868, particularly in the South. Very few Negroes were educated then.

Next, Warren dealt with the "separate but equal" doctrine, pointing out that there have been six cases in public education involving that concept (19). He added that, unlike some of those cases, equal facilities were not a problem. He stated:

> Our decision, therefore, cannot turn on merely a comparison of these tangible factors in the Negro and white schools involved in each of the cases. We must look instead to the effect of segregation itself on public education (20).

After indicating the importance of education, Warren posed the fundamental question:

> Does segregation of children in public schools solely on the basis of race, even though the physical facilities and other "tangible" factors may be equal, deprive the children of the minority group of equal educational opportunities (21)?

Warren then gave the Court's answer:

> To separate them from others of similar age and qualifications solely because of their race generates a feeling of inferiority as to their status in the community that may affect their hearts and minds in a way unlikely ever to be undone (22).
>
> We conclude that in the field of public education the doctrine of "separate but equal" has no place. Separate educational facilities are inherently unequal (23).

Before granting relief to the appellants, Warren requested that the parties present further argument on questions four and five:

> 4. Assuming it is decided that segregation in public schools violates the Fourteenth Amendment
> (a) would a decree necessarily follow that, within the limits set by normal geographic school districting, Negro children should forthwith be admitted to schools of their choice, or
> (b) may this Court, in the exercise of its equity powers, permit an effective gradual adjustment to be brought about from existing segregated systems to a system not based on color distinctions?
> 5. On the assumption on which questions 4 (a) and (b) are based,

and assuming further that the Court will exercise its equity powers to the end described in question 4 (b),
  (a) should this Court formulate detailed decrees in these cases;
  (b) if so, what specific issues should the decrees reach;
  (c) should this Court appoint a special master to hear evidence with a view to recommending specific terms for such decrees;
  (d) should this Court remand to the courts of first instance with directions to frame decrees in these cases, and if so what general directions should the decrees of this Court include and what procedures should the courts of first instance follow in arriving at the specific terms of more detailed decrees (24)?

Warren invited the United States Attorney General and the attorneys general of the states requiring or permitting segregation to submit briefs and appear as *amici curiae* in the further argument.

Case 5: Bolling v. Sharpe (1954). On the same day that the Court gave the *Brown* decision, the Chief Justice also delivered the opinion in *Bolling v. Sharpe (25).* This case tested the constitutionality of segregation in the District of Columbia. It was not treated with the *Brown* case, for it was not a challenge to state action, since the Fourteenth Amendment, governing *Brown,* restricts states, not Congress. Challenge in the *Bolling* case was thus made on the due process clause of the Fifth Amendment. The Bill of Rights, unlike the Fourteenth Amendment, does not include an equal protection clause.

In the District of Columbia the plaintiffs, Negro parents, charged that children were unlawfully excluded from Sousa Junior High School because of race. They maintained that nothing in the governing statutes empowered the board of education to operate separate schools for Negroes and whites. The Federal District Court granted a defense motion to dismiss the suit on the ground that the question of unequal facilities had not been raised. Then, before the Supreme Court, the justices were asked to reverse the dismissal and to rule on the constitutional issue.

In arriving at a decision, Warren discussed the due process and equal protection concepts. He said that the two terms "are not mutually exclusive," but that equal protection "is a more explicit safeguard of prohibited unfairness than 'due process of law *(26).*' " Warren stated further:

> Liberty under law extends to the full range of conduct which the individual is free to pursue, and it cannot be restricted except for a proper governmental objective. Segregation in public education is not reasonably related to any proper governmental objective, and thus it imposes on Negro children of the District of Columbia a burden that constitutes an arbitrary deprivation of their liberty in violation of the Due Process Clause *(27).*

SEGREGATION

The opinion provided for the case to be placed on the docket for reargument along with *Brown* on questions four and five.

Case 6: Brown v. Board (1955). In the reargument the United States, the parties, and Arkansas, Florida, North Carolina, Oklahoma, Maryland, and Texas participated. In the unanimous decision, *Brown v. Board of Education of Topeka (28)*, Chief Justice Warren, again speaking for the Court, gave the detailed decree as to how the previous *Brown* decision should be implemented. The Chief Justice indicated that both the local school officials and the district courts have responsibilities:

> Full implementation of these constitutional principles may require solution of varied local school problems. School authorities have the primary responsibility for elucidating, assessing, and solving these problems; courts will have to consider whether the action of school authorities constitutes good faith implementation of the governing constitutional principles. Because of their proximity to local conditions and the possible need for further hearings, the courts which originally heard these cases can best perform this judicial appraisal. Accordingly, we believe it appropriate to remand the cases to those courts *(29)*.

Warren then gave some guidelines to the district courts and spoke of the interest of the plaintiffs:

> In fashioning and effectuating the decrees, the courts will be guided by equitable principles. Traditionally, equity has been characterized by a practical flexibility in shaping its remedies and by a facility for adjusting and reconciling public and private needs. These cases call for the exercise of these traditional attributes of equity power. At stake is the personal interest of the plaintiffs in admission to public schools as soon as practicable on a nondiscriminatory basis *(30)*.

The Court directed that a "prompt and reasonable" start be made to comply with the 1954 *Brown* ruling. The justices also recognized that, once a start has been made, additional time may be required to provide for an effective implementation program. If this were needed, the Court held that the burden was upon the defendants to show that they were acting "in the public interest" and "consistent with good faith compliance" without unnecessary delay. Factors to consider in desegregation were:

> To that end, the courts may consider problems related to administration, arising from the physical condition of the school plant, the school transportation system, personnel, revision of school districts and attendance areas into compact units to achieve a system of determining admission to the public schools on a nonracial basis, and revision of local laws and regulations which may be necessary in solving the foregoing problems *(31)*.

Further, in explaining the role of the district courts, the opinion stated:

> They will also consider the adequacy of any plans the defendants may propose to meet these problems and to effectuate a transition to a racially nondiscriminatory school system. During this period of transition, the courts will retain jurisdiction of these cases *(32)*.

The Court then remanded the cases to the district courts which initially heard the cases where they were to:

> ... take such proceedings and enter such orders and decrees consistent with this opinion as are necessary and proper to admit to public schools on a racially nondiscriminatory basis with all deliberate speed the parties to these cases *(33)*.

Case 7: Pennsylvania v. Board (1957). Before the Supreme Court rendered any opinions after the *Brown* decisions about the standards of its segregation decisions, it extended its holding to clarify a private-public school relationship with the state. In so doing it brought private schools under state action where limited state involvement is concerned *(34)*.

The *Girard* case arose out of a will creating a trust fund for needy children. When Stephen Girard's will was probated after his death in 1831, a trust fund of $2,000,000 had been left to Philadelphia to operate a "college" for "poor white male orphans." The school now enrolls boys between the ages of six and ten and keeps them until they usually reach age eighteen. A regular educational curriculum plus ten trades is available to each student. The school opened in 1848. The city managed the operation of the school until 1869 at which time the job was turned over to the Board of Directors of City Trustees whose members were made agents of the city.

The school had an entirely white enrollment and was not challenged for admission by Negroes until February, 1954, when two boys applied. They were rejected, although they met all the school's qualifications except that they were colored. Suit was then begun against the board of directors, contending that exclusion of the students was in violation of the Fourteenth Amendment. The Pennsylvania Supreme Court denied relief.

The United States Supreme Court disposed of the case in a brief *per curiam* opinion, saying:

> The Board which operates Girard College is an agency of the State of Pennsylvania. Therefore, even though the Board was acting as a trustee, its refusal to admit Foust and Felder to the college because they were Negroes was discrimination by the State. Such discrimination is forbidden

by the Fourteenth Amendment. . . . Accordingly, the judgment of the Supreme Court of Pennsylvania is reversed and the cause is remanded for further proceedings not inconsistent with the opinion (35).

In order to comply with the Court's holding, the Orphan's Court was faced with two alternatives. It could either admit the Negro plaintiffs or replace the board of trustees with individuals acting as private citizens. The court chose the latter and selected thirteen trustees of the Girard estate whereupon the Supreme Court of Pennsylvania affirmed the action taken. The United States Supreme Court refused to review the state court decision. Finally, on September 11, 1968, four Negro boys enrolled at Girard College.

Litigation before the Court after this opinion has concerned the implementation of the *Brown* decisions. A review of the cases will be made before an analysis of them is given.

Case 8: Cooper v. Aaron (1958). The controlling case came four years after the first *Brown* decision in *Cooper v. Aaron (36)*. It arose out of a conflict in the Little Rock, Arkansas, school system in particular but concerned the entire state in general. The question was the validity of a delayed integration plan when violence threatens a school. The Supreme Court opinion gave attention to detailed facts of the case. The decision was unanimous, and all nine justices signed the opinion. In addition, Justice Frankfurter wrote a concurring opinion.

Following the 1954 *Brown* decision, the school board of Little Rock adopted a policy concerning desegregation. Under a plan submitted by the superintendent in May, 1955, integration would begin at the senior high school, follow at the junior high school, and be completed in the elementary schools. All levels would be desegregated by 1963. Initial integration was scheduled to start in 1957.

Negroes sought a more rapid program of integration and instituted litigation for relief. Both the District Court and the Court of Appeals upheld the school board plans. In the meantime, a 1956 amendment to the state constitution opposed the *Brown* decisions and did away with compulsory attendance at racially mixed schools.

When nine Negroes were scheduled to enroll at the white Central High School in Little Rock in 1957, real conflict began. The Governor dispatched the National Guard to the school to oppose integration, although the Supreme Court's findings pointed out that the action had not been requested, no crowds had gathered, and there were no threats of violence. In view of the Governor's action the school board requested the district court for instructions. The board was advised to proceed with desegregating the school. For three weeks the National

Guard stood shoulder to shoulder in preventing Negro students from enrolling. The District Court asked the United States Attorney General to fix responsibility for the interferences. Both the court and the Attorney General enjoined the Governor and the Guard from interfering with Negro admittance; so the guard was withdrawn.

On September 23 the nine Negroes entered school but later withdrew because of a hostile crowd. Two days later President Eisenhower sent federal troops to the school where they remained for two months. The federalized National Guard remained at the school the remainder of the year.

In February, 1958, the school board requested a postponement of the desegregation program and asked that the Negroes enrolled at Central High School be removed. Although the district court granted relief, the circuit court reversed. In special session convened on August 28, 1958, the Supreme Court heard the arguments of the case. On September 29, 1958, the Supreme Court affirmed the judgment of the circuit court. The Court, speaking through the Chief Justice:

> ... accepted without reservation the position of the School Board, the Superintendent of Schools, and their counsel that they displayed entire good faith in the conduct of these proceedings and in dealing with the unfortunate and distressing sequence of events which has been outlined. We likewise have accepted the findings ... that the educational progress of all the students, white and colored, of that school has suffered and will continue to suffer if the conditions which prevailed last year are permitted to continue.
> The significance of these findings, however, is to be considered in light of the fact, indisputably revealed by the record before us, that the conditions they depict are directly traceable to the actions of legislators and executive officials of the State of Arkansas, taken in their official capacities, which reflect their own determination to resist this Court's decision in the *Brown* case and which have brought about violent resistance to that decision in Arkansas (37).

Further, Warren added:

> The constitutional rights of respondents are not to be sacrificed or yielded to the violence and disorder which have followed upon the actions of the Governor and the Legislature. . . . Thus law and order are not here to be preserved by depriving the Negro children of their constitutional rights (38).

> In short, the constitutional rights of children are not to be discriminated against in school admission on grounds of race or color declared by this Court in the *Brown* case can neither be nullified openly and directly by state legislators or state executive or judicial officers, nor nullified indirectly by them through evasive schemes for segregation whether attempted "ingeniously or ingenuously (39)."

Next, the Court dealt with the assumption by the Governor and the

Legislature that they are not subject to the holding of *Brown*. Warren drew on *Marbury* v. *Madison* in holding that the judiciary is supreme. He added:

> It follows that the interpretation of the Fourteenth Amendment enunciated by this Court in the *Brown* case is the supreme law of the land, and Art. VI of the Constitution makes it of binding effect on the States "any Thing in the Constitution or Laws of any State to the Contrary notwithstanding." Every state legislator and executive and judicial officer is solemnly committed by oath taken pursuant to Art. VI, 1. 3, "to support this Constitution *(40)*."

Warren then reminded the defendants that no state official can "war against the Constitution without violating his undertaking to support it *(41)*."

Justice Frankfurter's concurring opinion dealt with the gravity of the problem. He condemned the state for interfering with the Little Rock school system and appealed for moral responsibility in supporting the *Brown* decisions.

Since *Cooper*, the Court has heard segregation cases either delaying integration or avoiding it by administrative schemes. The next cases following *Cooper* which involved the segregation question were *Goss* v. *Board of Education of Knoxville, Tennessee (42)* and *McNeese* v. *Board of Education (43)*, both decided on the same day.

Case 9: Goss v. *Board (1963)*. *Goss* concerned the legality of a transfer plan of the city of Knoxville. Under the arrangement school districts would be rezoned without reference to race. A student would be permitted "solely on the basis of his own race and the racial composition of the school to which he has been assigned by virtue of rezoning, to transfer from such school, where he would be in the racial minority, back to his former segregated school where his race would be in the majority *(44)*."

Justice Clark wrote the Court's unanimous opinion which answered the question if the transfer provisions deprived the Negroes of rights under the Fourteenth Amendment. At the outset Clark stated that if the plans operated solely on racial factors, the Court would strike them down. The Court's examination of the record indicated that race was the pivot on which the transfer plans worked. Clark said:

> While transfers are available to those who choose to attend school where their race is in the majority, there is no provision whereby a student might transfer upon request to a school in which his race is in a minority, unless he qualifies for "a good cause" transfer. . . . Here the right of transfer, which operates solely on the basis of a racial classification, is a one-way ticket leading to but one destination, *i.e.* the majority race of the transferee and continued segregation *(45)*.

Further in the opinion Clark stated:

> The recognition of race as an absolute criterion for granting transfers which operate only in the direction of schools in which the transferee's race is in the majority is no less unconstitutional than its use for original admission or subsequent assignment to public schools *(46)*.

> Not only is race the factor upon which the transfer plans operate, but also the plans lack a provision whereby a student might with equal facility transfer from a segregated to a desegregated school. The obvious one-way operation of these two factors in combination underscores the purely racial character and purpose of the transfer provisions. We hold that the transfer plans promote discrimination and are therefore invalid *(47)*.

In deciding if the provisions were unconstitutional, Clark said:

> In doing so, we note that if the transfer provisions were made available to all students regardless of their race and regardless as well of the racial composition of the school to which he requested transfer we would have an entirely different case. Pupils could then at their option (or that of their parents) choose, entirely free of any imposed racial considerations, to remain in the school of their zone or to transfer to another *(48)*.

The Court indicated that it might uphold transfer plans not based on racial factors and those allowing transfers to or from any school regardless of the race of the majority. Further, the Court regarded the following as valid conditions to support requests for transfer: (a) when a white student would otherwise be required to attend a school previously serving colored students only; (b) when a colored student would otherwise be required to attend a school previously serving white students only; and (c) when a student would otherwise be required to attend a school where the majority of students of the school or in his or her grade are of a different race *(49)*.

Case 10: *McNeese* v. *Board (1963)*. The *McNeese* case arising in Cahokia, Illinois, concerned the legality of the transfer of students by grades from one school to another. Litigation grew out of a reassignment of students due to an overcrowding of one of the predominantly white schools. At the Centreville school—97 per cent white—all pupils in the fifth and sixth grades were reassigned to a less populous school, all-Negro Chenot. At this school the reassigned students were kept segregated. The school enrollment consisted of 251 Negroes and 254 whites.

The Supreme Court granted *certiorari* while recognizing the Illinois Code which permitted fifty residents of a school district or 10 per cent —whichever is lesser—to file a complaint with the Superintendent of Public Instruction alleging that a pupil has been segregated due to race. The superintendent puts the complaint down for a hearing after which he requests the Attorney General to initiate a suit to remedy the practice. The courts may review any final decision of the superintendent. Under the school code, provision is also made wherein a school district may not file a claim for state aid unless it files a sworn statement that the district has complied with provisions outlawing segregation.

Justice Douglas wrote the opinion in which all justices joined except for Justice Harlan who dissented. Douglas said, in relying upon *Monroe* v. *Pope* for precedent:

> We have previously indicated that relief under the Civil Rights Act may not be defeated because relief was not first sought under state law which provided a remedy. . . .
> It is no answer that the State has a law which if enforced would give relief. The federal remedy is supplementary to the state remedy and the latter need not be first sought and refused before the federal one is invoked *(50)*.

Douglas held that federal law, not state law controls the case. He added:

> Nor is the federal right in any way entangled in a skein of state law that must be untangled before the federal case can proceed. For petitioners assert that respondents have been and are depriving them of rights protected by the Fourteenth Amendment. It is immaterial whether respondent's conduct is legal or illegal as a matter of state law. . . .
> Moreover, it is by no means clear that Illinois law provides petitioners with an administrative remedy sufficiently adequate to preclude prior resort to a federal court for protection of their federal rights *(51)*.

After he had examined the superintendent's role in effecting a remedy, Douglas concluded:

> Apparently no Illinois cases have held that the Superintendent has authority to withhold funds once he has received an affidavit from the district, even if he determines that the affidavit is false. In any event, the withholding of state aid is at best only an indirect sanction of Fourteenth Amendment rights. When federal rights are subject to such tenuous protection, prior resort to a state court proceeding is not necessary *(52)*.

Harlan's dissent was based on two factors. The Justice pointed out that Illinois had outlawed many years before the 1954 *Brown* decision both constitutional and statutory provisions for racial discrimination in the public schools. In commenting about his second objection, he said:

> The alleged discriminatory practices relate, rather, to the manner in which this particular school district was formed and the way in which the internal affairs of the school are administered. These are matters in which the federal courts should not initially become embroiled. Their exploration and correction, if need be, are much better left to local authority in the first instance *(53)*.

Case 11: Griffin v. *School Board (1964).* A year following the two previous decisions, the Supreme Court handed down another opinion which, like *Cooper,* concerned an attempt to forestall integration. *Griffin* v. *County School Board of Prince Edward County (54)* grew out of a plan by the county to close the public schools and operate a system of private schools. Litigation began in 1951 when a group of Negro children in Prince Edward County filed a complaint for their denial to attend a white school. The board of supervisors had decided in 1956 not to levy taxes or appropriate funds for integrated public schools. The Prince Edward School Foundation operated schools for white students with state financial assistance. When the case was brought before the courts, the district court held that public schools could not be closed while others remained open. The State Supreme Court held that the state constitution compelled neither the state nor the county to reopen the public schools in Prince Edward County or to furnish them funds. Prior to the Supreme Court decision, the Court of Appeals had vacated the judgment.

The Court, speaking through Justice Black, traced the history of the litigation. Black pointed out that the 1959 general assembly adopted a freedom-of-choice program, repealed the 1956 legislation, and made compulsory attendance a matter of local option.

The Court of Appeals in 1959 made three findings. It enjoined discriminatory practices in the county's schools. It instructed the county school board to take immediate steps to enroll students, without regard to race, at the white high school in September, 1959. Further, the board was directed to make plans to admit students to elementary and secondary schools without regard to race.

Schools of the county did not open in 1959, for the county supervisors levied no taxes for their support. White students attended private schools operated by the Prince Edward School Foundation. Whereas a school plant was built for the white students, the Negroes rejected an offer for a school. The school in 1959-60 was supported entirely by private contributions, whereas a year later the state legislature gave tuition grants varying from $125-$150 per pupil. The County Board of Supervisors also provided $100 for each child attending the private schools and granted deductions of up to 25 per cent for contributions to the school.

Besides the denial of equal protection, a supplemental complaint protested the payment of public funds to private schools excluding students on account of race. After reviewing the facts and stating the question, Black held:

> For reasons to be stated, we agree with the District Court that, under the circumstances here, closing the Prince Edward County schools while public schools in all the other counties of Virginia were being maintained denied the petitioners and the class of Negro students they represent the equal protection of the laws guaranteed by the Fourteenth Amendment (55).

Black then dealt with three facets of the case: (1) a petition to dismiss the supplemental question; (2) the major question of whether Negroes were denied equal protection of the law under the county's operation of schools; and (3) relief for the plaintiffs.

In dismissing the contention that the supplemental question was a new and separate course of action, Black held that the respondents' action was designed merely to circumvent integration. He pointed out that closing the school was county, not state, action. Another contention Black refused to accept was that the action was forbidden by the Eleventh Amendment. Finally, he reversed the judgment of the Court of Appeals in remanding the case and proceeded to the merits of the case.

Black next dealt with the primary question. The Supreme Court recognized the holding of the Court of Appeals in declaring valid the closing of Prince Edward's public schools and providing the tuition grants. The Court did not accept the reason for the closing, for the justices held that Negro children were denied equal protection of the laws. Black wrote that:

> Whatever nonracial grounds might support a State's allowing a county to abandon public schools, the object must be a constitutional one, and grounds of race and opposition to desegregation do not qualify as constitutional (56).

The third facet dealt with implementation decrees. Black indicated that:

> The Board of Supervisors has the special responsibility to levy local taxes to operate public schools or to aid children attending the private schools now functioning there for white children. The District Court enjoined the county officials from paying county tuition grants or giving tax exemptions and from processing applications for state tuition grants so long as the county's public schools remained closed. We have no doubt of the power of the court to give this relief to enforce the discontinuance of the county's racially discriminatory practices.... The injunction against paying tuition grants and giving tax credits while public schools remain closed is appropriate and necessary (57)....

Black added that:

> The time for mere "deliberate speed" has run out, and that phrase can

no longer justify denying these Prince Edward County school children
their constitutional rights to an education equal to that afforded by the
public schools in the other parts of Virginia *(58)*.

Justices Clark and Harlan joined in the Court's opinion except that
they disagreed with the holding that federal courts are empowered to
order the reopening of the schools.

Case 12: Rogers v. *Paul (1965).* In 1965 a brief *per curiam* opinion
was handed down by the Court in *Rogers* v. *Paul (59).* The case originating in Arkansas challenged the desegregation scheme operating at
the public high school of Fort Smith. Two Negro students brought
class action to integrate the white high school. Although one student
had already graduated and the other was in his senior year, the addition of parties to the suit was granted by the Court.

The school system's plan adopted in 1957 provided for the integration of one grade per year. In the fall of 1964, grades ten, eleven, and
twelve were still segregated. Negro petitioners were assigned to a Negro
school on the basis of race. The opinion held that:

> Pending the desegregation of the public high schools of Fort Smith according to a general plan consistent with this principle, petitioner and
> those similarly situated shall be allowed immediate transfer to the high
> school that has the more extensive curriculum and from which they are
> excluded because of race *(60).*

Petitioners challenged the assignment of faculty on a racial basis.
The Supreme Court overruled the Court of Appeals and held that the
petitioners had standing to make that challenge. Justices remanded for
a hearing on that matter. The justices explained:

> Two theories would give students not yet in desegregated grades sufficient interest to challenge racial allocation of faculty: (1) that racial allocation of faculty denies them equality of educational opportunity without regard to segregation of pupils; and (2) that it renders inadequate an
> otherwise constitutional pupil desegregation plan soon to be applied to
> their grades *(61).*

Justices Clark, Harlan, White, and Fortas would have set the case
down for argument and plenary consideration.

Case 13: Green v. *School Board (1968).* Three years elapsed before
the Supreme Court handed down another segregation decision. In this
appeal the justices were asked to overturn freedom-of-choice assignment
plans in three states. Rather than join the cases for one opinion as was
done in *Brown,* the Court, speaking through Justice Brennan, handed
down three separate opinions, each overruling the choice plans.

Green (62), Raney (63), and *Monroe (64)* were appealed respectively from the Fourth Circuit in Virginia, the Eighth Circuit in Arkansas, and the Sixth Circuit in Tennessee. The facts in each case were similar.

Originating in New Kent County, Virginia, the *Green* case attacked the assignment plan which provided for an individual to choose his own school. The fact situation revealed that the county, a rural area of 4,500 people had two schools, one each in the east and west. Half of the population was Negro. There was no residential segregation and no attendance zones for the school system. Buses traveled overlapping routes in serving New Kent, a white school and Watkins, a Negro school. Up until September, 1964, the schools had remained segregated, but in order to qualify for federal aid the local school board adopted a freedom-of-choice plan.

> Under that plan, each pupil may annually choose between the New Kent and Watkins schools and, except for the first and eighth grades, pupils not making a choice are assigned to the schools previously attended; first and eighth grade pupils must affirmatively choose a school *(65)*.

Justice Brennan noted that, even though the plan had been in operation for three years, no white child had elected to attend Watkins, and approximately 85 per cent of the Negro children still attended the Negro school. The Court ordered the local board of education to formulate a new plan.

The Court's reasoning was noted in the justices' assessment of the problems involved in desegregating a school system.

> There is no universal answer to complex problems of desegregation; there is obviously no one plan that will do the job in every case. The matter must be assessed in light of the circumstances present and the options available in each instance. It is incumbent upon the school board to establish that its proposed plan promises meaningful and immediate progress toward disestablishing state-imposed segregation. It is incumbent upon the district court to weigh that claim in light of the facts at hand and in light of any alternatives which may be shown as feasible and more promising in their effectiveness. Where the Court finds the board to be acting in good faith and the proposed plan to have real prospects for dismantling the state-imposed dual system "at the earliest practicable date," then the plan may be said to provide effective relief *(66)*.

The decision did not overrule all freedom-of-choice plans; rather the Court pointed out:

> We do not hold that "freedom of choice" can have no place in such a plan. We do not hold that a "freedom-of-choice" plan might of itself be unconstitutional, although that argument has been urged upon us. Rather, all we decide today is that in desegregating a dual system a plan utilizing "freedom of choice" is not an end in itself *(67)*.

Case 14: Raney v. Board (1968). The *Raney* case was an attack on a dual system in a rural county of Arkansas which, like New Kent, operated two schools. The school district served an area of eighty square miles; the two schools were ten blocks apart in the county's largest town, Gould. Totally segregated in 1964-65, the board of education adopted a freedom-of-choice plan to qualify for federal aid. Pupils could choose annually between Gould and Field Schools; those not making a choice would be assigned to the school previously attended. No white child had requested to attend Field, the Negro school, and only 15 per cent of the Negro children attended the predominantly white school, Gould.

During the first year of operation under the choice plan, twenty-eight Negroes were denied transfer due to lack of available space. At the same time that litigation arose over the assignment plan, the school board made plans to replace the high school building at Field. The petitioners then sought an injunction to enjoin construction at that site rather than at the Gould location.

The District Court dismissed the complaint. Without actually deciding where the new building should be located, the Supreme Court remanded the case to the District Court, with two charges: "(1) that a constitutionally acceptable plan is adopted, and (2) that it is operated in a constitutionally permissible fashion so that the goal of a desegregated, nonracially operated school system is rapidly and finally achieved *(68).*"

Case 15: Monroe v. Board (1968). Like the two previous cases, *Monroe* was a challenge to freedom of choice but it included also a free transfer plan. The city of Jackson, Tennessee, operated thirteen schools—eight elementary, three junior high, and two senior high schools.

After the *Brown* decision, Tennessee enacted a pupil placement law which, due to the limited amount of integration, was not upheld by the District Court. In 1963, the local school board adopted a modified plan providing for the automatic assignment of a pupil to a school within his attendance zone and allowing for transfer to another school of his choice, space permitting. Since the school did not operate buses, the student would have to provide his own transportation.

When relief was first sought in 1964, the three Negro elementary schools had no white children and 118 Negro pupils were enrolled in four of the five formerly all-white elementary schools.

The District Court found discrimination in two instances: (1) The Board of Education had denied Negro children the right of transfer.

(2) The attendance zones had been gerrymandered to retain racial identities.

In 1964 the faculties and staff were segregated.

The Court, relying primarily upon *Green,* held that the plan perpetuated segregation, in that some schools still remained completely segregated while there was limited integration in others. The school board was ordered to formulate a new plan which would remove racial distinctions.

Case 16: United States v. *Montgomery County Board of Education (1969).* The last decision in education of the Warren Court involved a plea to desegregate a school faculty in Montgomery County, Alabama. Evidence showed that the state had made no effort for ten years to integrate the public schools.

The instant action *(69)* was begun in 1964 by Negro children and their parents with the United States as *amicus curiae.* The record showed that a dual system was in effect in Montgomery and that faculty were assigned to schools according to race.

A local federal district judge ordered integration of certain grades to begin in September 1964 which resulted in eight Negroes' being transferred to white schools. (In 1963-64 there were approximately 15,000 Negro children and 25,000 white children.)

Since 1964, there had been yearly proceedings, opinions, and orders by the district court judge. The record showed an increasing recognition of the intent of the local school board to desegregate, even though more rapid progress could have been made.

Judge Johnson's 1968 order provided for safeguards that would insure that new school buildings would not be constructed so as to perpetuate segregation. There were other provisions acceptable to the local school board. Only one provision was challenged, that related to faculty and staff desegregation of Jefferson Davis High School. Faculty integration had been ordered in 1966-67, but progress had not been made. Judge Johnson then set a minimum standard in which the ratio of white to Negro faculty members would be "substantially the same as it is throughout the system." For full-time teachers for the 1968-69 school year, the judge held that:

> ... each school with fewer than 12 teachers was required to have at least two full-time teachers whose race was different from the race of the majority of the faculty at that school, and in schools with 12 or more teachers, the race of at least one out of every six faculty and staff members was required to be different from the race of the majority of the faculty and staff members at that school *(70).*

Goals for ensuing years were not specifically stated.

The Court of Appeals struck down that part of the order that set a specific goal for 1968-69 and modified it to provide for "substantially or approximately" the 5:1 ratio earlier decreed. The Court also held that more flexible standards should be applicable to faculty desegregation.

Justice Black, speaking for the United States Supreme Court, held that:

> The modifications ordered by the panel of the Court of Appeals, while of course not intended to do so, would, we think take from the order some of the capacity to expedite, by means of specific commands, the day when a completely unified, unitary, nondiscriminatory school system becomes a reality instead of a hope (71).

The orders of Judge Johnson of the District Court were to stand.

Black stated that "We do not . . . argue here that racially balanced faculties are constitutionally or legally required (72)." In passing, he noted that both parties to the case were interested in desegregating the schools; in this case it was simply a matter of determining to what degree. The real interest of the Supreme Court was in assuring that the spirit and intention of the *Brown* decisions be followed.

Relief

The Supreme Court decisions striking down segregation in higher education granted immediate relief. However, the *Brown* cases, unlike the earlier ones, involved many more students and affected the structure of society more profoundly. The justices, in delaying a year to give the implementation decision, may have recognized that a sudden, drastic integration of the schools might have upset the social structure of the South. They may have assumed also that, given some time, the South would assume sufficient leadership responsibility to implement the Court order without further directives.

Both parties to the case offered their positions respecting an implementation of the 1954 *Brown* decision. The Negro plaintiffs held that their constitutional rights were personal and present and demanded direct, immediate admission to the white schools. The defendant states refused to recognize that the Court had the authority to issue decrees which, in their opinion, were matters for them to settle. The United States Attorney General took a position between the two opposing parties. Whatever course of action was to be taken, the constitutional rights had to be given to the Negro parties which the *Brown* decision proclaimed, and it would be done with a minimum of injury to the persons affected. How could this be achieved? Several approaches could be taken.

One approach would be the ending of segregation immediately as the appellants urged in the 1953 reargument and which they believed should be ordered at the time of the decision. This was done in Delaware. Forces opposing this idea cited possible antagonism in the South and the possible psychological harm that could be done to Negroes attending school in a hostile atmosphere.

A second approach would have been the gradual ending of segregation according to a plan devised by the Supreme Court. Such a plan might be uniform for all school systems; such an approach might give the Court a legislative function.

The Court could have decided to end segregation gradually according to a plan directed by a master appointed by the Court. The Court could exercise overall supervisory functions while allowing the master to handle the details. This plan might have the advantage of being flexible or adaptable to local school systems. This would permit adjustments to local attitudes toward segregation.

In handing down the decree through the second *Brown* decision, the Court took a position between the extremes of both parties to the case. Moreover, it actually refrained from following any of the three alternatives. Although progress had already been made in the District of Columbia, Kansas, and Delaware, only South Carolina and Virginia were, in actuality, affected by the decrees. Yet, the Court spoke for all.

Certain advantages accrued because the cases were class actions. This type of action is permitted in suits wherein persons affected by the suit are so numerous that it would be impractical for all to appear in court, but it does allow one suit for all persons similarly affected. The right sought involves a common question of law; it seeks a common relief. In the segregation cases the "class" was the Negro children. The common question of law dealt with racial segregation and equality; the relief asked was an end to segregated school facilities for the Negro children. In a class action those not directly involved in the litigation are subject to the same conditions of relief as are the plaintiffs in the case.

In the class actions, the plaintiffs felt that they could gain more favorable support in the integration proceedings. Any chance for mootness would be less likely to occur, and the possibility of compromise by the parties would be diminished.

Not only was this a class action case, it was a case in equity. This means that the Court has the responsibility of fashioning a remedy by giving orders directly to the parties involved. The orders may entail specified conditions of compliance; failure to obey can bring action for contempt. In giving the orders, the justices placed responsibility upon the local school authorities who would be expected to assume the initiative for complying with the Court's order. As if recognizing ahead of time that the transition might encounter problems, the Court stated that "additional time may be necessary to carry out the relief in an effective manner *(73)*." The problem, however, was one of intention since the Court fashioned no strict rules to guide local school authorities. The opinion suggests that patience and understanding must guide the parties. Indication of the Court's strong feeling of cooperation with the decision is revealed in the statement that "It should go without saying that the vitality of these constitutional principles cannot be allowed to yield simply because of disagreement with them *(74)*." Thus, time to work out the problem in a constructive manner is one thing, the justices recognized, while delaying tactics are another problem.

That the Supreme Court gave such authority to the local units to fashion implementation decrees reaffirmed the recognition of the autonomy given to local school units. The Court did this without compromising any principles. According to Garber, the Court:

> ... left in the hands of the states a matter that, historically, belongs there—the matter of assuming the responsibility for operating their own school systems within the constitutional framework. What more could the court have done? It gave a definite answer as it saw it *(75)*.

School boards were instructed to make a "prompt and reasonable start toward full compliance" with the 1954 *Brown* ruling. However, the flexibility of the implementation could vary among and within states. The several obstacles cited by the Court are the actual determinants of the rate of progress to be made. The courts stand by as watchdogs to make certain that reasonable efforts are being made. If a local board can assure to the satisfaction of the court that it is acting in good faith and with reasonable speed in overcoming these obstacles, the court may be hesitant in interfering with the board's desegregation program.

Since compliance rested with the federal district courts, two courses of action were open to them. The courts could compel obedience to the 1955 *Brown* holding by punishing or threatening to punish offenders. These courts had a responsibility of overturning measures designed to forestall desegregation plans. What such measures could they expect?

Resistance patterns might take several forms. (1) A school system could refuse to desegregate or wait until the courts forced it to do so. It could tie up the courts with practices designed to stall as long as possible. (2) State segregation laws could be enacted wherein desegregated schools would not receive state funds. (3) Assignment plans could be made wherein a school board selected each pupil individually to attend a school. Such factors as health, general welfare, and achievement could be criteria for placement. (4) Another tactic could be the creation of free "private" education. Since the Fourteenth Amendment limits states, not individuals, private schools would not be affected by the *Brown* decisions. (5) As a last resort, the state might abolish its schools and offer no aid.

In reflecting on the relief granted, Garber states:

> As has been stated, the court directed the states to end the practice of segregating their pupils in public schools within a "reasonable" time. Thus it refrained from fixing a deadline and, probably more important than that, it refrained from creating a hard and fast national pattern or procedure to be followed in erasing the "color line" in public schools. The reasoning followed by the court in arriving at this conclusion is significant. It reasoned that, in achieving the constitutional principles enunciated, numerous local problems may be encountered. School authorities are the agencies vested with the responsibility for solving these problems and should be given the opportunity of so doing but courts must consider whether these authorities act in good faith in implementing the constitutional principles *(76)*.

Delay in Compliance

Timing of the 1954 *Brown* decision worked to the advantage of both the Supreme Court and school officials who were affected. It allowed summer for school personnel to begin plans for compliance, and it afforded time for persons antagonistic to the decision to adjust to its holding. It also made the Supreme Court's assignment of administering relief easier, for in the meantime, the District of Columbia and Kansas announced plans to integrate, and Delaware soon followed with integration plans.

The Department of Justice had suggested a delay of compliance, but the Supreme Court ignored its two suggestions. One would have been to integrate on a school-by-school basis; the other, to integrate on a grade-by-grade basis beginning with the first grade.

When the Court did not grant immediate relief, it did not set a precedent. Reasonable time for compliance was granted by the Court as early as 1907 when no specified time was ordered for a copper company to cease discharging noxious fumes *(77)*. In 1910 a Court decree gave Standard Oil Company an extension of up to six months *(78)*. A like time was given American Tobacco Company one year later *(79)*. However, in the previous school segregation cases, the relief sought was immediately given.

Recognizing the importance of time in complying with the decision, former Attorney General Rogers wrote:

> The problems are difficult at best but they become hazardous if the underlying intent of those who are opposed to the decision of the court—particularly those in official positions who are opposed to the decision—is one of defiance . . . time and understanding are necessary ingredients to any long term solution. But time to work out constructive measures in an honest effort to comply is one thing; time used as a cloak to achieve complete defiance of the law of the land is quite another *(80)*.

In *Brown*, 1955, the Supreme Court took a position that relief was not necessarily immediate even though one's rights to equal protection had been denied. It reaffirmed this position in *Cooper* in outlining the role of the federal district courts pursuant to the guidelines of the second *Brown* case. While holding that relief to many Negro students would be immediate, the Court also stated:

> Of course, in many locations, obedience to the duty of desegregation would require the immediate general admission of Negro children, otherwise qualified as students for their appropriate classes, at particular schools. On the other hand, a District Court, after analysis of the relevant factors (which, of course, excludes hostility to racial desegregation), might conclude that justification existed for not requiring the present non-segregated admission of all qualified Negro children *(81)*.

In *Brown* of 1955 and *Cooper* the Court did not indicate how long a delay of integration it would sanction. One problem arising from court-approved plans is the degree of enjoyment of personal rights by the Negro plaintiffs. Under a program of gradual desegregation, some Negro students could be denied the right or opportunity of attending school with white students. This is conceivable when court-approved desegregation plans come too late for those students who will have already completed their public school education. Especially does this hold on a grade-a-year plan which starts with the first grade. However, the problems created by *Brown* were very different from those involving university students. *Brown* involved millions of students whereas the other cases involved individuals. The Court thus sought to provide for an orderly transition without overturning completely the school systems.

While in its earlier pronouncements the Court was reluctant to set any time limit for desegregation, it has in later cases been less patient with delays. In *Goss* Justice Clark, in noting the "good faith compliance" and "all deliberate" guides of the 1955 *Brown* decision stated:

Now, however eight years after this decree was rendered and over nine years after the first *Brown* decision, the context in which we must interpret and apply this language to plans for desegregation has been significantly altered *(82).*

More specifically, Black stated one year later in *Griffin:*

The time for mere "deliberate speed" has run out, and that phrase can no longer justify denying these Prince Edward County school children their constitutional rights to an education equal to that afforded by the public schools in the other parts of Virginia *(83).*

Rogers also pointed out a time factor. The justices held that petitioners were entitled to immediate relief, that a grade-a-year plan of integration was too slow.

Equal Treatment

The Fourteenth Amendment prohibits states from discriminating unfairly against racial groups; it does not restrict discrimination by private citizens. The Amendment does not grant to Congress the authority to enact legislation against private injustice, although it does circumscribe public injustice. In the series of segregation cases between *Plessy* and *Brown* the Court suggested that the "separate but equal" doctrine was invalid. The *Brown* case clearly enunciated the principle that segregation denied the plaintiffs the equal protection of the law.

Since the federal Constitution leaves education largely to the states, state autonomy is of major import. The schools are governed by constitutional as well as statutory provisions. The Fourteenth Amendment with its equal protection clause, however, does not require that the states give identical treatment to all persons. It does require, on the other hand, that legislation which differentiates groups in treatment must be based on relevant and legitimate distinctions. Moreover, the treatment accorded each group must be reasonable and germane to the object sought or the purpose of the legislation itself. Segregation based entirely on color does not meet the constitutional test of relevancy and legitimacy.

Like the equal protection clause of the Fourteenth Amendment, the due process clause of the Fifth Amendment requires that government accord like treatment to all persons unless some reason justifies unlike treatment. In the segregation cases the Court had to decide if Negroes were actually treated alike when sent to a school comparable to or equal in facilities, but designated only for Negroes. If that were answered negatively, the Court then had to decide if the character of the Negro pupils justified the inequality. The justices found the treatment unequal; they held that race was an insufficient reason for the differences in treatment.

In public education separate but equal facilities violate the principle of equal protection, for separate school facilities still generate inequality. Therefore, schools, as instrumentalities of the state, must be open to people without racial distinctions. The Court giving this opinion consisted of justices from all sections of the country and from the two major political parties. The opinion is an expansion of the Court's previous holdings in *Sweatt* and *McLaurin* which dealt with university enrollment.

The *Brown* decision recognizes that segregation within itself denotes the inferiority of the Negro race. Warren said:

> To separate them from others of similar age and qualifications solely because of their race generates a feeling of inferiority as to their status in the community that may affect their hearts and minds in a way unlikely ever to be undone *(84)*.

Since segregation denotes inferiority, the Court reasoned, it affects one's motivation to study and to learn.

The language of both *Brown* and *Bolling* indicates that the Court has overruled schools' segregating without regard for actual findings of inherent inequality. Both cases hold that segregation on the basis of race in public education is not related to any governmental objective; any classification to the contrary denies the majority equal protection and liberty without due process of law.

Since a state cannot cause feelings of inferiority due to race, it cannot enforce a policy of segregation. The Court holds, then, that a child cannot be refused admission to a school on the grounds that only children of the white race can attend that school. That holding does not apply when a child attends an integrated school, for then the state is not a party in causing a feeling of inferiority due to race.

Intangible Factors

In treating the *Brown* case of 1954, the Supreme Court was asked to deal directly with the "separate but equal" doctrine. The justices elected not to follow either of two choices. They could have recognized that schools are instrumentalities of the state, and the state must make its services available to all people—being, in part, "color blind." They could have followed the same reasoning used in the graduate school cases by examining whether or not the schools in question were equal. Rather than deal with either of those approaches the Court considered the intangible factors, holding that segregation itself creates a feeling of inferiority to the Negro race.

When the Court disposed of the "separate but equal" doctrine, it recognized that segregation was segregation against the Negro and not mutual segregation between the Negroes and the whites. This caused the Negro to suffer pangs of inferiority resulting from his race and prevented his sharing educational experiences with students of the white race. The justices recognized that this was detrimental to the learning process. These conditions being created by compulsory segregation, the separation of the races was not necessary to achieve a legitimate governmental objective. The 1954 *Brown* decision stated:

> Segregation of white and colored children in public schools has a detrimental effect upon the colored children. The impact is greater when it has sanction of the law; for the policy of separating the races is usually interpreted as denoting the inferiority of the negro group. A sense of inferiority affects the motivation of a child to learn. Segregation with the sanction of law, therefore, has a tendency to . . . [retard] the educational and mental development of negro children and to deprive them of some of the benefits they would receive in a racial(ly) integrated school system (85).

To substantiate its holding in the case the Court made use of data which did not necessitate the specific overruling of *Plessy* v. *Ferguson*. Social scientists who testified at the hearing maintained that segregation is harmful to the Negro child. Their presentation was related to the broad question of the effect of segregation on Negro learning rather than to the effects on the immediate children involved. Footnote eleven of the *Brown* decision indicates the Court's authority for its holding (86).

The lower courts of both Virginia and South Carolina rejected the evidence of sociologists as being irrelevant. The courts of Kansas and Delaware relied on the testimony in their fact-finding but held it to be irrelevant under the *Plessy* doctrine. Neither *Brown* nor *Bolling* mentions the scientific data which were used extensively in the lower courts. Neither case refers either to the statement made by thirty-two psychologists and sociologists as an appendix to the plaintiff's brief before the Supreme Court. The only reference made by the Court was recognition of the nonlegal data in a quotation from the Kansas and Delaware cases with a reference to authorities in footnote eleven.

Precedent for the use of nonlegal data in arriving at decisions antedates the Warren Court. As early as 1905 the Court relied on economic evidence in deciding the validity of hours regulating the banking industry *(87)*. Very elaborate briefs were prepared by Louis Brandeis— later appointed a justice of the Court—for the Court in *Muller* v. *Oregon (88)* in 1908 when medical and sociological facts pointed out the evils of working conditions not subject to regulations.

Discussion of the questions propounded by the Court were inconclusive, the justices felt; furthermore, previous segregation cases did not aid in the instant case. In *Cumming* and *Gong Lum* the separate-but-equal doctrine was not an issue. The college cases dealt with separate but equal factors whereas in the instant case the Court found that facilities had been or were in the process of being equalized. Warren stated that:

> Our decision, therefore, cannot turn on merely a comparison of these tangible factors in the Negro and white schools involved in each of the cases. We must look instead to the effect of segregation itself on public education *(89)*.

The Court, without citing legal precedent, then dealt with the importance of education. The justices recognized a national interest in a child's schooling by citing (1) compulsory attendance laws, (2) expenditure of money, (3) education as a necessity for performing basic public responsibilities, (4) the need for schooling for the performance of good citizenship, (5) an awakening of cultural values, (6) preparation for professional training, and (7) aid in adjustment *(90)*.

The Court felt that state-imposed segregation so affects the relationships of white and Negro students that it prevents educational interaction. Consequently, children are denied an opportunity for stimulation and competition which they will face later in life. It is this factor that "damages the hearts and minds and ability of Negro children to learn and brands them as inferior in the public mind," the Court stated. A student's isolation from major educational developments results in his receiving an inferior education. This isolation makes educational equality impossible under the Fourteenth Amendment.

State Action

State action covers a broad spectrum of activity. It includes the laws passed by a state, but also much more. It also includes action under the authority of state law. State officials, municipal and county officials, and school administrators in the performance of their duties come under state action. Within the meaning of the Fourteenth Amendment, school officials act as the state; hence their action is considered to be state action. In the segregation cases the Supreme Court has enunciated the principle that state action in deliberately operating the public schools on a segregated basis is in violation of the rights of Negroes. Even though the state is the source of the discrimination, it cannot be the final determiner of the disposition of a segregation case. The federal Constitution was controlling since the plaintiffs alleged an injury under the equal protection clause of the Fourteenth Amendment.

Although the Fourteenth Amendment bars discrimination against state action, it does not mean that all discrimination is illegal, for the Amendment does not control private action. Thus, one may choose his social acquaintances by any standard he wishes. However, when the state becomes involved, the matter is no longer social but political. A state cannot act as an individual in discriminating against its citizens. What distinctions are made must be real and pursuant to a proper governmental purpose, race not being one of those factors.

Insistence by the Supreme Court that schools treat white and Negro students without distinction to race does not expand the Court's role in other areas of the school such as the curriculum. Nothing in the opinions suggests that the Court intended to alter any distinction between governmental and non-governmental action. The control of education remains with the states, for the opinion does not redistribute state and local functions.

The Court expanded the concept of state action in the *Girard* ruling. A question in the case was the extent, if any, to which state action was involved in the operation of an essentially private school. The Court held that the school was not really private in that the trustees were agents of the city. The city being a creature of the state, the Girard school was, in effect, bound by the same holding as were the other schools affected by *Brown*. This is recognition that a school need not be entirely involved in a governmental function and be less subject to governmental restrictions as would be applied to schools entirely public. If the state is the source of the racial discrimination, then it becomes subject to the equal protection of the Fourteenth Amendment. The case built against *Girard* by the Negro plaintiffs showed state action in the following ways: (1) The board actually manages the college. (2) Governmental officials appoint the school administrators. (3) Governmental officials are *ex officio* members of the board. (4) The legislature regulates the method of selection of the managing body. (5) Annual reports are made to a governmental body. (6) Governmental agents audit the books *(91)*.

The plaintiff's case was held to be stronger than that of the defense. The latter held that the city contributes no money to Girard and that any discrimination results from the requirements of a private citizen rather than from the state. The Supreme Court opinion does not indicate the degree to which the justices were influenced by any, all, or none of the claims or whether they arrived at an opinion independent of the claims.

Another question pertinent to the case was the honoring of a will. The plaintiff's attorneys argued that state action was involved, while the defendants maintained that Girard's wishes were clear and should be respected since one may will his property as he wishes.

A general rule holds that one may will his property as he wishes; however, a will cannot be enforced if it is contrary to existing law. Since the Supreme Court recognized that the trustees were agents of the state, the Court saw discrimination—contrary to law.

The *Girard* case was decided on a narrow point, that the state may not permit its officials or agencies to promote discrimination. The real relationship of Girard College and the state is that the state is the source of discrimination when it allows its facilities to be used for racially discriminatory purposes. The real issue, therefore, was not the admission of Negro students to the school but the role of the trustees in managing the school.

Girard extends *Brown* in that it shows that the Supreme Court will not sanction any form of assistance by a state agency in furthering discrimination in the schools. According to Shanks, the position of the states is the following:

> For once it is established that there are some cases in which the state may not allow its courts to be used to impose discrimination, it would seem that it may not permit its facilities as trustee to be used to carry out a discriminatory scheme.
>
> Thus, despite the fact that Girard supplied all the funds for the College and despite the fact that he decreed the discriminatory practice, the state is the effective source of the discrimination if it allows its facilities to be used to carry out the plan. This, then, is the significance of the relationships and contacts between Girard College and the state. When the state allows its managerial facilities to be used to operate a discriminatory scheme, state action results *(92).*

Cooper reaffirmed the state's role in educating children, and Chief Justice Warren gave no intention of the Court's desire to take away any of the state's authority. On the other hand, he recognized that the states have a positive duty to operate within the bounds of constitutional authority. He said:

It is, of course, quite true that the responsibility for public education is primarily the concern of the States, but it is equally true that such responsibilities, like all other state activity, must be exercised consistently with federal constitutional requirements as they apply to state action *(93)*.

Whereas the state has a positive duty to provide for the education of children, it may not abrogate its duty as was shown in *Griffin*. That opinion showed that a state cannot delegate to the counties those governmental functions which would promote discrimination. There, equal protection was denied Negroes when the state abandoned its public school system in Prince Edward County, allowed the county to operate its schools, but provided financial support. In looking at the reason for closing the schools, Justice Black said:

But the records in the present case could not be clearer that Prince Edward's public schools were closed and private schools operated in their place with state and county assistance, for one reason, and one reason only: to ensure, through measures taken by the county and the State, that white and colored children in Prince Edward County would not, under any circumstances go to the same school. Whatever nonracial grounds might support a State's allowing a county to abandon public schools, the object must be a constitutional one, and grounds of race and opposition to desegregation do not qualify as constitutional *(94)*.

Racial Classifications

Before the 1954 *Brown* decision the previous Supreme Court opinions had not specifically decided that racial classifications were unconstitutional. This decision, however, gave a direct answer, for the litigation was a challenge to state constitutions and statutes which classified students entirely on the basis of race.

All laws classify and, as such, discriminate. For instance, most states do not allow persons under age twenty-one to vote. The United States Constitution, however, forbids unreasonable or discriminatory classification. An unreasonable classification is one having no relationship between what it creates and a governmental objective. A discriminatory classification is one wherein one class of people is made to feel inferior. A federal census asking for the race of persons being interrogated would be neither unreasonable nor discriminatory. The Court opinion in *Brown* of 1954 sets forth the principle that classification of pupils in schools according to race is invalid. That which promotes an injustice resulting from the separation of racial groups by a state is prohibitive, for whenever a school system attempts to keep the Negro separated from whites simply because he is a Negro, that school is operating in violation of the equal protection clause of the Fourteenth Amendment.

The 1954 *Brown* decision involved state constitutions and statutes which required or permitted classification on the basis of race. It was concerned only with the assignment of children in the public schools on race rather than on any other factor. In the *Bolling* decision the Court's pronouncement is more striking when it holds that segregation is not properly related to any governmental objective. When the Court held in *Bolling* that due process of law prevents federal discrimination based on race, it was the first time that the Court had overturned congressional action on this basis.

Blaustein and Ferguson state:

> While equal protection does not require absolute equality, it does require some kind of equality. The distinction between permissible and prohibited inequality in legislation has been measured by the reasonableness test which recognizes the validity of discriminatory legislation where (and only where) there are real differences between the subjects classified *(95)*.

The 1954 *Brown* position, augmented by *Girard*, holds that any racial classification whose existence could in any way be connected with the state is unconstitutional. The subsequent cases confirm and strengthen that holding.

Overthrow of Plessy

When Warren stated that "in the field of public education the doctrine of 'separate but equal' has no place," he did not state that *Plessy* v. *Ferguson* was specifically overruled. The opinion neither criticized nor approved decisions from *Plessy* and afterward. Reference to *Plessy* was made concerning psychological effects of segregation. Warren added that "Any language in *Plessy* v. *Ferguson* contrary to this finding is rejected *(96)*." The Court implied that *Plessy* had become outdated in 1954. Public education had grown considerably since 1896 and the *Plessy* decision to a very large-scale operation in the mid-twentieth century. This necessitated a new look at the Fourteenth Amendment.

The Court's opinion in 1954 did not state that *Plessy* was decided erroneously, either on the basis of legal precedent or because of a conflict with history; neither did the opinion overturn *Plessy* by following later decisions. The Court did indicate that changing conditions and new developments in learning and psychology prompted a new look at segregation in education.

Without specifically saying so, the Court substituted Justice Harlan's dissent in 1896 for the majority opinion in *Brown*. It was Harlan who stated that the Constitution was color blind. Under the *Plessy* doctrine the opinion which allowed the states to compel separation of the races was a conditional one. Segregation was permissible only if the facilities were equal. Built into this principle was an implied warning that compulsory separation would be reevaluated if equality were not maintained. Thus, the people maintaining segregation would be responsible for the degree of political freedom given them by the Court. That freedom would be determined by both history and experience.

In holding to its decision, the Chief Justice did not rely on the extensive and confusing evidence which was compiled while Congress adopted the Fourteenth Amendment, nor did Warren base the decision on precedents of earlier cases, although he referred to them. What he did do was to point out the many changes in education occurring since 1868 and 1896. The opinion is, in effect, an agreement with Harlan's dissent. Whereas in five previous segregation cases, the decisions were reached without deciding specifically if a state racial classification was unconstitutional *per se*, the *Brown* decision answered this in the affirmative. It holds to the proposition that when personal rights are an issue under the Constitution, the meaning depends upon the interpretation of conditions and situations existing rather than conditions at the time of the adoption of that part of the Constitution.

Standards of Desegregation

The first case in which the Supreme Court rendered a decision regarding standards of compliance with the *Brown* decisions was *Cooper v. Aaron*, decided four years after the first *Brown* case. Although the Court was asked to rule on only one narrow point—that is, whether public hostility to a school board's plans for desegregation is reason enough for a delay—the justices dealt with some broader aspects of the desegregation problem. Speaking through the Chief Justice, the Court asserted that no scheme to avoid segregation would be tolerated, whether attempted "ingeniously" or "ingenuously."

In announcing the decision, the Court not only gave an opinion but stated a mood affecting the federal system. The dicta were a reminder to the defendants that state officials, upon assuming office, take an oath to support the United States Constitution. No state official of any branch of government can oppose the Constitution without violating his oath to support it. *Cooper* recognized that the executive and the legislative branches of the government of Arkansas had not felt a responsibility to obey the federal court orders and that such disregard for the Constitution can do nothing but undermine the federal system. Implicit in the oath taken by officials is the understanding that decisions of the Supreme Court will be accepted and followed, including the segregation decisions. Since state officials may not escape this decree, they are bound to follow through with a program of desegregation.

When the Court emphasized that the constitutional rights of school children were not to be interfered with because of race or color, the justices sought to enlarge upon a narrow decision. The decision prohibited the opening of schools on any factor other than nonsegregation, and it restrained school authorities from using funds, property, or facilities for the conduct of "private" schools.

To circumvent the Court's holdings, some Southerners, in opposition to the segregation decisions, advanced a proposal to redefine the state's role in education. In some states compulsory school attendance laws were repealed and talk of cutting off state aid to desegregated schools persisted. Leasing of schools to "private" groups was also suggested. The most radical proposal was to abolish the state's school systems. Involved in this plan was a government subsidy through some financial means.

Two cases before the Supreme Court confirmed the feeling of many that the "private" schools were in effect public schools. In *Cooper* the Court spoke out that:

> State support of segregated schools through any arrangement, management, funds, or property cannot be squared with the Amendment's command that no State shall deny to any person within its jurisdiction the equal protection of the laws (97).

In the *Prince Edward* case the Court also spoke about the abandonment of the public schools. After the Court of Appeals had invalidated legislation which closed integrated schools and cut off state aid, Virginia refused to give direct support to Prince Edward County. This forced the closing of the schools beginning in 1959. Justice Black held for the Supreme Court that:

> closing the Prince Edward County Schools while public schools in all the other counties of Virginia were being maintained denied the petitioners

and the class of Negro students they represent the equal protection of laws guaranteed by the Fourteenth Amendment *(98)*.

In *Cooper* the Court recognized that the responsibility for operating the public schools lies with the state but added that a corresponding trust dictates action consistent with federal constitutional and statutory principles. The opinion stated:

> It is, of course, quite true that the responsibility for public education is primarily the concern of the States, but it is equally true that such responsibilities like all other state activity, must be exercised consistently with federal constitutional requirements as they apply to state action. The Constitution created a government dedicated to equal justice under law. The Fourteenth Amendment embodied and emphasized that ideal *(99)*.

The opinion in *Cooper* stated that the Court would tolerate no scheme of discrimination by the state against Negroes seeking attendance at white schools. Additionally, a delay in implementation of the Court's order would be denying the Negroes their constitutional rights. Therefore, the enactment of state legislation for the purpose of evading or delaying the application of the Court's order would not meet the position taken by the justices in *Cooper*.

Paul writes that:

> The boards are to begin with a "prompt and reasonable" start and finish as soon as practicable; there can be "geographical variation" between states and within each state; and in deciding on what must be done and how soon in any given area we must determine the scope of the "administrative" problems confronting the board and perhaps too, the scope of the "community attitudes" problems. The magnitude of these "obstacles" in any given locality will determine the rate of progress to be made in that locality toward the ultimate objective. If a local board can do enough to satisfy a court of its good faith in its "assessment" and proposed solution of these; i.e. if it can demonstrate the intent to effect compliance by overcoming the "obstacles" to desegregation within a reasonable time, then the court may be reluctant to interfere with the board's desegregation program although asked to do so by some group of dissatisfied parent plaintiffs *(100)*.

Chief Justice Warren underscored the feeling of the justices in *Cooper* in several ways. He announced that all nine members were joint authors of the decision. He added that three new justices—Harlan, Brennan, and Whittaker—had joined the Court since the 1954 decision and stated that they were in agreement with the original decision.

In the *Prince Edward* case Black's opinion held to the standard that a state cannot circumvent the Court's ruling by setting up socalled private schools, its being a denial of equal protection of the law.

Black pointed out that accreditation of the schools is one factor to be considered. He added:

> Apart from this expedient, the result is that Prince Edward County school children, if they go to school in their own county, must go to racially segregated schools, which, although designated as private, are beneficiaries of county and state support *(101).*

Black acknowledged and reaffirmed that a state has considerable latitude in passing laws and in deciding whether the laws shall operate in specified counties or in all of them. He stated:

> But the record in the present case could not be clearer that Prince Edward's public schools were closed and private schools operated in their place with state and county assistance, for one reason, and one reason only: to ensure, through measures taken by the county and the State, that white and colored children in Prince Edward County would not, under any circumstances, go to the same school. Whatever nonracial grounds might support a State's allowing a county to abandon public schools, the object must be a constitutional one, and grounds of race and opposition to desegregation do not qualify as constitutional *(102).*

Guidelines set by the Court in the *Goss* case added another dimension. The justices held that desegregation through nonracial residential zoning could not be upheld. The justices saw that in the plan the perpetuation of segregation wherein students in a racial minority in a school would have been allowed to transfer to a school in which they were in a racial majority could not be sustained.

Likewise, in *Green, Raney,* and *Monroe,* the Court looked, not so much at the desegregation plans themselves, but rather at the end result of those plans. When it was shown that in each instance a freedom-of-choice system effected very little positive action toward integration, the Court overruled the validity of those plans. The justices were apparently letting school officials know that choice plans are legal if they integrate the schools.

Compulsory Integration of the Races

Brown recognized that public schools as agencies of the states are bound by the Fourteenth Amendment against discriminatory state action. *Bolling* held that the federal Congress was bound by the Fifth Amendment to refrain from discriminatory practices in the schools of the District of Columbia. The two decisions raise the question of whether the schools are required to integrate. The two cases did not decree that states must mix persons of different races in the public schools. The justices held, however, that a state may not deny to any

SEGREGATION

child the right to attend a school solely on the basis of race. Milbourn writes:

> The Constitution does not forbid such segregation as results from voluntary action, and no violation of the Constitution results solely because de facto segregation creates a school which is for all practical purposes segregated. The children of a minority race have no constitutional right to have white children attend classes with them in the public schools. . . . Therefore, in the absence of qualifying factors there is no affirmative legal duty to integrate the schools as a whole, or to take steps to nullify fortuitous segregation resulting from residential patterns *(103)*.

Milbourn's position is taken by Kauper who writes:

> Moreover, the decision does not mean that the states are required to establish school districts in such a way as to insure racial integration. The Fourteenth Amendment does not require states to take steps to force the two races together *(104)*.

Sanders states:

> The facts and holding of these cases do not indicate that the Constitution requires a compulsory intermingling in the sense of complete integration of all educational facilities regardless of individual choice. Rather under the fact patterns the decision is to the effect that race is not a constitutionally valid basis for the exclusion from public schools of an otherwise qualified applicant who desires to use such facilities. Obviously the decision does not invalidate the good-faith setting up of classifications, on such accepted bases as sex, intelligence, and choice of educational program when made applicable without regard to race *(105)*.

The Fourteenth Amendment prohibits states from denying anyone the equal protection of the laws, but it does not compel the states to force integration. So long as the laws are applied equally to both races, the courts are satisfied. For example, if factors such as geography or transportation cause the races to be separated, the courts would not compel integration. Segregation is forbidden, but integration is not required.

In the 1955 *Brown* case the Court did not use the word "segregation" except in the footnote which repeated questions four and five. The text of the opinion used the word "discrimination" five times and "nondiscriminatory" three times. Reference is made in the decision, not to the objectives of the legislation, but to motives of the legislators. The Supreme Court decisions holding that a law discriminates have been found on the grounds that the legislators have acted out of a motive to perpetuate segregation. Taken together, the two *Brown* cases mean that laws based on racial classifications are discriminatory and, as such, are unconstitutional.

Sedler states that:

> The statement of "no duty to integrate" is true so far as it goes, but represents a generalization rather than a sound analysis of the Court's holding. The most accurate observation in the above quotation is that "no general reshuffling of the schools in any school system has been commanded." That is what is meant by the fact the board is not required to integrate. It does not have to completely alter school boundaries and to insure that every school district is mixed, even though some students will have a great distance to travel. Of course this does not mean that the board may not decide to fully integrate the schools as a matter of social and educational policy; it merely means that the holding in *Brown* does not require it to do so *(106)*.

According to Sedler, there are two conditions operating in situations of actual segregation. One is where the board of education could establish an integrated school, but has not done so, even though no serious harm would likely result. The other condition is the operation of a segregated school by choice due to the racial concentration within that area.

"No duty to integrate" is really more of a defense mechanism than a constitutional principle. If the segregation decisions do not require an affirmative duty to integrate, then the burden of proof rests with the local school officials to show that racial classifications are not used in assignment of children to school.

Summary

Since 1954 the Supreme Court has decided several cases affecting segregation in the public schools. In none of these decisions was the holding more noteworthy than in the 1954 *Brown* case outlawing segregation by race in the public schools. This opinion affected schools in more than one-third of the states. Subsequent cases have dealt with plans for ending segregation and with litigation arising from delay and circumvention of the Court's decisions. A brief summary of each case follows.

Brown et al. v. Board of Education of Topeka et al. (1954) (107). State constitutions and statutes which provide for the segregation of children in the public schools on the basis of race are in violation of the equal protection clause of the Fourteenth Amendment. This decision outlawed long-standing practices of operating dual school systems for whites and Negroes.

Bolling v. Sharpe (1954). Segregation by race of public school students in the District of Columbia is in violation of the due process clause of the Fifth Amendment, for it is not related to a governmental objective.

Brown et al. v. Board of Education of Topeka et al. (1955). This decision effectuated a decree of relief under the previous *Brown* decision by remanding the cases to the federal district courts. Responsibility for desegregation rests with local school officials who are charged to proceed with plans consistent with local administrative problems.

Pennsylvania et al. v. Board of Directors of City Trusts of the City of Philadelphia (1957). A private school is, in fact, subject to the 1954 *Brown* decision when there is state action in the institution's operation. Since the school in question has its board of directors chosen by the city, it is subject to the state action concept.

Cooper et al., Members of the Board of Directors of the Little Rock, Arkansas, Independent School District, et al. v. Aaron et al. (1958). Violence or the threat of violence does not suspend one's constitutional rights when desegregation is concerned. Further, state officials may not abrogate their responsibility of assisting in school desegregation without violating their charge to uphold the United States Constitution.

Goss v. Board of Education of Knoxville, Tennessee (1963). A school transfer plan operating on racial factors is unconstitutional.

McNeese v. Board of Education of Cahokia, Illinois (1963). Under the federal Civil Rights Act, one does not have to exhaust state remedies before seeking relief in a federal court.

Griffin v. County School Board of Prince Edward County (1964). A state may not allow a county to close its schools while permitting schools in other counties to remain open. Race is not a constitutional reason for closing schools.

Rogers v. Paul (1965). Desegregation of schools on the basis of a-grade-a-year is too slow in that it denies some children the opportunity to attend an integrated school.

Green v. School Board (1968). A freedom-of-choice plan in Virginia perpetuated segregation and thus was in violation of the Fourteenth Amendment.

Raney v. Board (1968). Assignment plan in Arkansas resulted in a dual system and was held to be unconstitutional.

Monroe v. Board (1968). The Court struck down a freedom-of-choice plan, including free transfer provisions, on the grounds that the schools remained segregated.

United States v. Montgomery County Board of Education (1969). The Court upheld a federal district court faculty integration plan at a fixed ratio.

In these decisions the voting of the justices is an indication of their agreement in interpreting the Constitution as giving equal protection to all persons, particularly Negro school children. In the sixteen cases studied in this chapter, there was only one major dissent, that of Justice Harlan in *McNeese.*

Four of the decisions were written by Chief Justice Earl Warren. Further, those he wrote—the two *Brown* cases, *Bolling*, and *Cooper*— were actually the most significant in that they declared segregation in schools to be unconstitutional, announced the relief, and provided clarification of desegregation proceedings. The general agreement of the justices in the decisions may indicate the strong positive position taken by the Court in eliminating school segregation.

The segregation cases are significant Supreme Court decisions in that they affected large numbers of people and met with bitter opposition. Persons critical of the opinions forecast an encroachment by the Court in local school affairs. However, the decisions have not upset the fabric of federal-state-local relationships. In *Brown, Cooper,* and *Griffin* the Court emphasized the proper relationship of the states and the local school districts in directing their educational programs. At the same time the justices have emphasized that attempted circumvention of their decisions will be struck down.

In arriving at the initial *Brown* decision, the Supreme Court relied on sociological as well as legal factors. However, this is not a revolutionary approach as the Court used nonlegal data almost fifty years earlier.

Decisions involving segregation have turned on the equal protection clause of the Fourteenth Amendment, an exception being *Bolling*, decided on the due process clause of the Fifth Amendment. As interpreted by the Supreme Court, equal protection means, in fact, equal treatment or no separation of students by schools according to race. Equal treatment implies one's associations with many persons and with varied situations one may expect to encounter as an adult. A segregated school does not serve this purpose.

In outlawing segregation the Court at the outset granted a reasonable time for school officials to resolve administrative problems. However, the more recent cases indicate a lack of patience when the justices note that the time for "deliberate speed" has passed.

Notes to Chapter IV

1. *Plessy* v. *Ferguson*, 163 U.S. 537, 544 (1896).
2. *Ibid.*, p. 545.

SEGREGATION

3. *Missouri ex rel. Gaines* v. *Canada, Registrar of the University of Missouri, et al.*, 305 U.S. 337 (1938).
4. *Sipuel* v. *Board of Regents of the University of Oklahoma et al.*, 332 U.S. 631 (1948).
5. *McLaurin* v. *Oklahoma State Regents for Higher Education et al.*, 339 U.S. 637 (1950).
6. *Ibid.*, p. 641.
7. *Sweatt* v. *Painter et al.*, 339 U.S. 629 (1950).
8. Harry S. Ashmore, *The Negro and the Schools* (Chapel Hill: University of North Carolina Press, 1954), p. 49.
9. *Brown et al.* v. *Board of Education of Topeka et al.*, 347 U.S. 483 (1954).
10. *Brown*, 344 U.S. 1 (1952).
11. *Brown*, 344 U.S. 141 (1952).
12. *Brown*, 345 U.S. 792 (1953).
13. *Brown*, 98 F. Supp. 797 (1951).
14. *Briggs* v. *Elliott*, 103 F. Supp. 920 (1952).
15. *Davis* v. *County School Board of Prince Edward County*, 103 F. Supp. 337 (1952).
16. *Gebhart* v. *Belton*, 91 A. (2d) 137 (1952).
17. "High Court Bans School Segregation; 9-to-0 Decision Grants Time to Comply," *The New York Times*, CIII, No. 35, 178 (May 18, 1954), 14.
18. *Brown*, 345 U.S. 972 (1953).
19. *Cumming* v. *Board of Education of Richmond County*, 175 U.S. 528 (1899); *Gong Lum et al.* v. *Rice et al.*, 275 U.S. 78 (1927); *Missouri* v. *Canada*, 305 U.S. 337 (1938); *Sipuel* v. *Oklahoma*, 332 U.S. 631 (1948); *Sweatt* v. *Painter*, 339 U.S. 629 (1950); *McLaurin* v. *Oklahoma State Regents*, 339 U.S. 637 (1950).
20. *Brown, op. cit.*, p. 492.
21. *Ibid.*, p. 493.
22. *Ibid.*, p. 494.
23. *Ibid.*, p. 495.
24. *Brown*, 345 U.S. 973 (1953).
25. *Bolling et al.* v. *Sharpe et al.*, 347 U.S. 497 (1954).
26. *Ibid.*, p. 499.
27. *Ibid.*
28. *Brown et al.* v. *Board of Education of Topeka, et al.*, 349 U.S. 294 (1955).
29. *Ibid.*, p. 299.
30. *Ibid.*, p. 300.
31. *Ibid.*
32. *Ibid.*, p. 301.
33. *Ibid.*
34. *Pennsylvania et al.* v. *Board of Directors of City Trusts of the City of Philadelphia*, 353 U.S. 230 (1957).
35. *Ibid.*, p. 231.
36. *Cooper et al., Members of the Board of Directors of the Little Rock, Arkansas, Independent School District, et al.* v. *Aaron et al.*, 358 U.S. 1 (1958).
37. *Ibid.*, p. 14.
38. *Ibid.*, p. 16.
39. *Ibid.*, p. 17.
40. *Ibid.*, p. 18.
41. *Ibid.*, p. 18.
42. *Goss et al.* v. *Board of Education of Knoxville, Tennessee, et al.*, 373 U.S. 683 (1963).

43. *McNeese et al. v. Board of Education for Community Unit School District 187, Cahokia, Illinois, et al.*, 373 U.S. 668 (1963).
44. *Goss, op. cit.*, p. 684.
45. *Ibid.*, p. 686.
46. *Ibid.*, p. 688.
47. *Ibid.*
48. *Ibid.*, p. 687.
49. *Ibid.*, p. 686.
50. *McNeese, op. cit.*, p. 671.
51. *Ibid*, p. 674.
52. *Ibid.*, p. 676.
53. *Ibid.*, p. 677.
54. *Griffin et al. v. County School Board of Prince Edward County et al.*, 377 U.S. 218 (1964).
55. *Ibid.*, p. 225.
56. *Ibid.*, p. 231.
57. *Ibid.*, p. 232.
58. *Ibid.*, p. 234.
59. *Rogers et al. v. Paul et al.*, 382 U.S. 198 (1965).
60. *Ibid.*, p. 199.
61. *Ibid.*, p. 200.
62. *Green et al. v. County School Board of New Kent County et al.*, 391 U.S. 430 (1968).
63. *Raney et al. v. Board of Education of the Gould School District et al.*, 391 U.S. 443 (1968).
64. *Monroe et al. v. Board of Commissioners of the City of Jackson et al.*, 391 U.S. 450 (1968).
65. *Green, op. cit.*, p. 433.
66. *Ibid.*, p. 439.
67. *Ibid.*
68. *Raney, op. cit.*, p. 449.
69. *United States v. Montgomery County Board of Education*, 395 U.S. 225 (1969).
70. *Ibid.*, p. 232.
71. *Ibid.*, p. 235.
72. *Ibid.*, p. 236.
73. *Brown*, 1955, *op. cit.*, p. 300.
74. *Ibid.*
75. Lee O. Garber, "U.S. Supreme Court Takes Middle of the Road on Segregation," *The Nation's Schools*, LVI (July, 1955), 72.
76. *Ibid.*
77. *Georgia v. Tennessee Copper Company*, 206 U.S. 230 (1907).
78. *Standard Oil Company v. United States*, 221 U.S. 1 (1910).
79. *United States v. American Tobacco Company*, 221 U.S. 106 (1911).
80. William P. Rogers, "The Problem of School Segregation: A Serious Challenge to American Citizens," *American Bar Association Journal*, XLV (January, 1959), 24.
81. *Cooper, op. cit.*, p. 7.
82. *Goss, op. cit.*, p. 689.
83. *Griffin, op. cit.*, p. 234.
84. *Brown*, 1954, *op. cit.*, p. 494.
85. *Ibid.*

86. *Ibid.*
87. *Lochner* v. *New York*, 198 U.S. 45 (1905).
88. *Muller* v. *Oregon*, 208 U.S. 412 (1908).
89. *Brown*, 1954, *op cit.*, p. 492.
90. *Ibid.*, p. 493.
91. Hershel Shanks, " 'State Action' and the Girard Estate Case," *University of Pennsylvania Law Review*, CV (December, 1956), 230.
92. *Ibid.*, p. 237.
93. *Cooper, op. cit.*, p. 19.
94. *Griffin, op. cit.*, p. 231.
95. Albert P. Blaustein and Clarence Clyde Ferguson, Jr., *Desegregation and the Law* (New Brunswick, New Jersey: Rutgers University Press, 1957), p. 121.
96. *Brown*, 1954, *op. cit.*, p. 494.
97. *Cooper, loc. cit.*
98. *Griffin, op. cit.*, p. 225.
99. *Cooper, loc. cit.*
100. James C. N. Paul, "The Litigious Future of Desegregation," *Educational Leadership*, XIII (October, 1955), 110.
101. *Griffin, op. cit.*, p. 230.
102. *Ibid.*, p. 231.
103. Don L. Milbourn, "De Facto Segregation and the Neighborhood School," *Wayne Law Review*, IX (Spring, 1963), 516.
104. Paul G. Kauper, "Segregation in Public Education: The Decline of *Plessy* v. *Ferguson*," *Michigan Law Review*, LII (June, 1954), 1151.
105. Paul H. Sanders, "The School Segregation Cases: A Comment," *Vanderbilt Law Review*, VII (August, 1954), 995.
106. Robert Allen Sedler, "School Segregation in the North and West: Legal Aspects," *Saint Louis University Law Journal* VII (Spring, 1963), 251.
107. This also includes *Briggs* v. *Elliott*, *Davis* v. *County School Board*, and *Gebhart* v. *Belton*.

Chapter V

ACADEMIC FREEDOM

Introduction

The concept of academic freedom has grown out of a tradition that in colleges and universities there must be independent thought and unobstructed teaching necessary for the continuance of learning and growth of the institution. Constitutionally, academic freedom is thought of as a right of the freedom of speech and press guarantee of the First Amendment.

By definition, academic freedom is, according to Stevenson:

> the unrestrained opportunity for every qualified scholar to follow, within the standards imposed by his profession, his inquiry for truth wherever his imagination, intelligence, and integrity lead him, coupled with the right to state his views as findings and have their validity tested by critical examination and discussion (1).

Hoffman's definition states that academic freedom is:

> ... (a) the freedom of professionally qualified persons to inquire into, discover, interpret, publish, and teach the truth as they see it within the field of their competence and the freedom to do these things without being pressured, penalized, or otherwise molested by authorities or other persons within or without their institutions of learning; (b) the right of students to be taught of unconstrained instructors and to have access to all available data pertinent to their subjects of study at an appropriate educational level; and (c) the right of teachers, researchers, and students to exercise the freedoms constitutionally guaranteed to all citizens (2).

There are sufficient differences between the colleges and the public schools to affect the nature and the degree of academic freedom. The backgrounds of the students within a school are more diverse below the college level. The composition of the school faculty is likely to be representative of the community, and the subjects in the curriculum are reflective of the interests of the students.

Students in the public schools necessitate a different approach to instruction. The young, immature student must be taught with some restraint until he can reach a stage of responsible maturity. His instruction centers around the transmission of the cultural heritage, the prevailing attitudes, and the unquestioned facts. As one approaches maturity, he begins independent inquiry and criticism. Until that stage, however, the child is more closely supervised and instructed by the teacher. The average child of school age spends more daylight hours with his teachers than he does with his parents. He cannot help being impressed by his instructors, whether for good or bad. The teacher's character, personality, and interests naturally influence the child.

The community is directly tied in with the public school. The parents of school children are aware of and interested in what is being taught. The school patrons expect much of their teachers. Does this mean, however, that the community should place restrictions on its teachers? Does it mean that a teacher is expected to restrain himself in his teaching, his activities, and his beliefs? Is the teacher expected to fit into a mold devised by the community?

An expected by-product of academic freedom is the emergence of the non-conformist. The existence of such a person raises some questions. What limits may be placed on the freedom of teachers? How much freedom may be allowed in a period of tension? When does nonconformity become disloyalty or subversion?

It is recognized that the United States Constitution does not guarantee public employment, that teaching is a privilege and not a right. Yet, public employment cannot be controlled by unconstitutional restrictions. The First and the Fourteenth Amendments have within recent years included academic freedom within their rights guaranteed to citizens. The first recognition of academic freedom as constitutionally protected speech came in Justice Douglas's dissent in *Adler* v. *Board of Education.* Douglas said:

> I cannot for example find in our constitutional scheme the power of a state to place its employees in the category of second-class citizens by denying them freedom of thought and expression. The Constitution guarantees freedom of thought and expression to everyone in our society. All are entitled to it; and none needs it more than the teacher *(3).*

The United States Supreme Court has heard few cases in recent years touching on academic freedom of the public school teacher. Those heard by the Warren Court deal principally with two problems: statutes curbing teachers' association and oaths affecting their loyalty. It is these two primary areas of academic freedom that this chapter treats. Two additional cases touch on the freedom of pupils in the public schools.

The Cases Involving Freedom of Association of Teachers

The concept of the right of association is fundamental to a democratic society. Yet, this right is directly mentioned neither in the United States Constitution nor in the constitutions of the fifty states. Association as a constitutional right has developed from the right of assembly of the First Amendment and has been protected by the due process clause of the Fourteenth Amendment. Thus, the right is a constitutionally protected freedom from invasion by both the national and the state governments. But, under some conditions, government may limit or regulate this right in order to protect other rights. The requirements of the public order and safety may restrict this freedom.

Since World War II there has been an increasing concern over subversive organizations and activities in this country. To combat this concern, the federal and state governments have enacted legislation placing restrictions on freedom of association. Typically, the statutes require persons to provide information about their associations. The restrictive elements of the statutes prompt several questions. May a state, committed to democratic principles, curb an individual's liberty through the company he keeps? May a state punish an individual for keeping undesirable company? When does an individual's right of association yield to the interests of the state?

One danger of restricting the right of association is that Americans may become overly conscious about affiliating with organizations that may be only partly acceptable to most persons. The end result could be the lessening of one's effectiveness and the subsequent lack of growth of a democratic society.

To what extent may government set standards for its teachers affecting their right of association? To what extent shall disclosures be made to school officials? At the outset, it is recognized that there must be a minimum standard in public employment. If an employee of the public knowingly belongs to a subversive organization, some feel that the teacher, faced with questions about or evidence of his membership, should not remain silent and still be retained on the payroll. Others feel that a teacher should not be subjected to restrictions not placed on other citizens.

Some teachers who have been called before investigating committees have invoked the Fifth Amendment as a protection against self-incrimination. Their refusal to submit answers prompts two questions. Does the plea indicate that the person is unfit to teach? Is the refusal to answer or give evidence against himself or his friends an indication of actual guilt, or a moral conviction?

Case 1: Slochower v. Board (1956). Refusing to cooperate with those making the interrogation makes the teacher more likely to be dismissed and to have his reputation scarred. The victim might ask if such consequences should follow if he exercised his privilege of invoking the Fifth Amendment. The matter of dismissal reached the Supreme Court in *Slochower v. Board of Higher Education of New York City (4).* The case turned on a statute providing that whenever any employee of the city invoked the Fifth Amendment in questions about his official conduct, he would be immediately released from his position. Slochower was employed as a professor of German at Brooklyn College which was supported from city funds. Although Slochower was not employed by the public schools, he was subject to Section 903 of the City Charter as were the elementary and secondary teachers. In this case it was the reach of the statute, not the position of the teacher in question.

At a Senate investigating committee hearing devoted to subversive influences in American education, Slochower refused to answer all questions about his associations. He testified that he was not a member of the Communist Party, and he answered questions about his beliefs and associations since 1941. He refused, however, to tell if he had held membership in the Communist Party in 1940-1941.

Although he was entitled to tenure, Slochower was soon dismissed after the hearing. He claimed that his discharge was a violation of due process and equal protection of the Fourteenth Amendment. He contended that Section 903 of the New York City Charter, under which he was dismissed, was unconstitutional in that it made no provision for a hearing.

The Board of Faculty based its position upon two claims: answering the questions would tend to prove Slochower guilty; avoiding an answer would cause him to invoke falsely the privilege against self-incrimination. The Kings County Supreme Court upheld Slochower's dismissal, upheld also by the Appellate Division and the Court of Appeals. Slochower then appealed to the United States Supreme Court.

Through Justice Clark's majority opinion, the Court considered only the due process claim. In analyzing the questions asked, Slochower, the Court reasoned that:

> In practical effect the questions asked are taken as confessed and made the basis of the discharge. No consideration is given to such factors as the subject matter of the questions, remoteness of the period to which they are directed, or justification for exercise of the privilege. It matters not whether the plea resulted from mistake, inadvertence or legal advice

conscientiously given, whether wisely or unwisely. The heavy hand of the statute falls alike on all who exercise their constitutional privilege, the full enjoyment of which every person is entitled to receive (5).

The Court's problem, Clark asserted, was balancing the state's interests with the individual's rights. In this case the latter was paramount. The Court recognized a person's right to invoke the Fifth Amendment and that guilt should not be presumed in exercising the privilege. It serves, Clark said, "to protect the innocent who otherwise might be ensnared by ambiguous circumstances (6)." The justices made it clear, however, that the city may inquire into the fitness of a teacher. It is, nonetheless, a different matter when, under the present inquiry, investigation was not directed toward the property, affairs, or government of the city. The Court also noted that the Board of Faculty had possessed for twelve years the information the investigating committee sought. The summary dismissal of Slochower without a hearing thus was a violation of due process of law. The judges added, however, that:

This is not to say that Slochower has a constitutional right to be an associate professor of German at Brooklyn College. The State has broad powers in selection and discharge of its employees, and it may be that proper inquiry would show Slochower's continued employment to be inconsistent with a real interest of the State (7).

Justices Burton and Minton concurred in a dissent written by Reed. They held that the city should have the authority to require facts of its employees relative to official conduct. The investigation, they maintained, was conducted by a legally constituted body. Failure to supply the answers to such questions constituted grounds for dismissal.

Justice Harlan's dissent was premised on the condition that the investigation was pertinent toward insuring the qualifications of a good teacher. He indicated that people have a lack of confidence in their schools when teachers refuse to answer questions about their official conduct. The teachers then become no longer suitable for public school teaching.

The majority opinion did not indicate what the components of a proper hearing should involve. Its holding was limited to the ruling that a teacher's dismissal based upon facts necessarily involved in a hearing, violates due process without the hearing.

Case 2: Sweezy v. New Hampshire (1957). In 1957 the Supreme Court heard another case dealing with freedom of association. *Sweezy v. New Hampshire* (8) concerned the power of the state to compel a teacher to disclose the contents of a lecture and to delve into his political associations.

Six justices agreed on a decision but could not agree on the reasoning leading to the opinion. Chief Justice Warren wrote the plurality opinion in which Justices Black, Douglas, and Brennan concurred. Justice Harlan concurred in an opinion written by Justice Frankfurter. Justice Burton joined Clark in a dissent, while Whittaker took no part in the case.

Sweezy resulted from a 1951 statute of the New Hampshire legislature making all "subversive persons" ineligible for employment by the state government or as teachers in public schools and colleges. To implement the act, the legislature empowered the attorney general to make investigations about suspected violators. Sweezy was indicted after delivering a guest lecture at the University of New Hampshire.

While being questioned by the attorney general, Sweezy discussed his past conduct and associations. He testified that he had never been a member of the Communist Party and that he had not advocated overthrow of the government by force or violence. He refused to respond to interrogation about his knowledge of and affiliation with the Progressive Party. Sweezy also refused to reveal the contents of his lecture at the university. After his second appearance before the attorney general in June, 1954, Sweezy was sentenced to jail for contempt.

After disposing of the facts in the case, Chief Justice Warren discussed the role of investigations as they affect one's associations in education. The Chief Justice said:

> There is no doubt that legislative investigations, whether on a federal or state level, are capable of encroaching upon the constitutional liberties of individuals. It is particularly important that the exercise of the power of compulsory process be carefully circumscribed when the investigative process tends to impinge upon such highly sensitive areas as freedom of speech or press, freedom of political association, and freedom of communication of ideas, particularly in the academic community *(9)*.

Warren talked further about academic freedom and association:

> Merely to summon a witness and compel him, against his will, to disclose the nature of his past expressions and associations is a measure of governmental interference in these matters. These are rights which are safeguarded by the Bill of Rights and the Fourteenth Amendment. We believe that there unquestionably was an invasion of petitioner's liberties in the areas of academic freedom and political expression—areas in which government should be extremely reticent to tread.
>
> No field of education is so thoroughly comprehended by man that new discoveries cannot yet be made. Particularly is that true in the social sciences, where few, if any, principles are accepted as absolutes. Scholarship

cannot flourish in an atmosphere of suspicion and distrust. Teachers and students must always remain free to inquire, to study and to evaluate, to gain new maturity and understanding; otherwise our civilization will stagnate and die *(10)*.

The Court held that a legislative committee could not cross-examine a teacher on the contents of his lecture or on the interpretation and classification of material used in the classroom. Warren condemned the procedure used, stating that the mandate given the attorney general was so broad as to amount to a denial of due process of the Fourteenth Amendment. In effect, reasoned the Court, what the legislature had done was to ask the attorney general to do its work for it. This practice was deplored as investing too much authority in the attorney general. The Court was unable to decide if the questions posed by the attorney general were those the legislature wanted answered.

Frankfurter took issue with Warren's position of the separation of legislative and executive functions. In Clark's dissent, he and Burton maintained that the state should be able to investigate the extent of subversive activities. Hamilton commented:

> Although much of what is said in the opinion relates to universities, there is little doubt that in a similar case the court would accord similar freedom to those who teach the social studies in the public schools. This does not mean that all social science teachers are given carte blanche to question and throw doubts upon our governments and institutions and to advocate vicious or crackpot changes. Academic freedom has never been held to be unrestrained license *(11)*.

While the Court held that the teacher is free from legislative interference, it did not limit the authority of the educational institutions to supervise teachers. The opinions of Warren and Frankfurter revealed that protection is given to academic freedom under the First and Fourteenth Amendments. *Sweezy* does not indicate that all investigatory power is denied simply because education is involved.

Case 3: Beilan v. Board (1958). The year after *Sweezy* was decided, the Court heard a case in which a public school teacher appealed for freedom of association and for the freedom to refrain from revealing that association. Like the two previous cases, *Beilan v. Board of Public Education, School District of Philadelphia (12)*, represented an effort to get a teacher to answer questions about his political affiliations. Beilan, having taught in Philadelphia for twenty-two years, was called by his superintendent to answer questions about his alleged affiliation with the Communist Political Association in 1944. In a private interview with the superintendent on June 25, 1952, Beilan sought permission to seek counsel before answering. On October 14, 1952, Beilan, when asked again by the superintendent if he had been an officer in the Communist Party, declined to answer that and similar questions. Thirteen months later he invoked the Fifth Amendment before the Subcommittee of the Committee on Un-American Activities of the House of Representatives.

The superintendent and the school board fired Beilan for incompetency. They made it clear, however, that Beilan's loyalty was not an issue. His dismissal was for refusal to answer questions about his activities, not about the activities themselves.

The Pennsylvania Supreme Court upheld the dismissal as being justified when Beilan refused to answer his superintendent's questions. The justices refused to look beyond that.

The United States Supreme Court divided 5-4, the majority upholding the state supreme court. Three dissenting opinions were written. The majority accepted the belief that Beilan's refusal to answer questions amounted to insubordination, which was incompetency and grounds for dismissal according to the Pennsylvania School Code. The majority quoted *Horosko* v. *Mt. Pleasant School District (13)*, a case originating in Pennsylvania, where it was held that a teacher no longer holding the respect of the community may be dismissed for incompetency.

Justice Burton wrote the majority opinion. He said, in part:

> By engaging in teaching in the public schools, petitioner did not give up his right to freedom of belief, speech or association. He did, however, undertake obligations of frankness, candor and cooperation in answering inquiries made of him by his employing Board examining into his fitness to serve it as a public school teacher. . . .
> The question asked of petitioner by his Superintendent was relevant to the issue of petitioner's fitness and suitability to serve as a teacher. . . . The Board based its dismissal upon petitioner's refusal to answer any inquiry about his relevant activities—not upon those activities themselves. It took care to charge petitioner with incompetency, and not with disloyalty.
> We find no requirement in the Federal Constitution that a teacher's classroom conduct be the sole basis for determining fitness. Fitness for teaching depends on a broad range of factors *(14)*.

Beilan could not challenge his dismissal on the grounds of remoteness of the 1944 activities, for the superintendent had stated clearly that there were other questions to ask, which Beilan indicated he would refuse to answer.

Burton referred to *Slochower* and made a distinction between the two cases. It is one thing, Burton pointed out, for city officials to interrogate a teacher and another for officials to discharge a teacher for refusing to answer questions not related to affairs of the city. In

Beilan no inference was taken from the teacher's refusal to answer.

Frankfurter wrote a concurring opinion. He felt that Beilan's discharge was because:

> ... governmental authorities, like other employers, sought to satisfy themselves of the dependability of employees in relation to their duties. Accordingly, they made inquiries that, it is not contradicted, could in and of themselves be made. These inquiries were balked. The services of the employees were therefore terminated *(15)*.

Frankfurter then called for some restraint in solving school matters. He wrote:

> I am not charged with administering ... the school system of Pennsylvania. The Fourteenth Amendment does not check foolishness or unwisdom in such administration. The good sense and right standards of public administration in those States must be relied upon for that, and ultimately the electorate *(16)*.

Chief Justice Warren based his dissent upon the argument that Beilan's invoking the Fifth Amendment was involved in the school board's dismissing him, a position which Brennan took in a separate dissent. Justice Douglas, with whom Black concurred, expressed alarm over government's penalizing a citizen for his beliefs and associations. He indicated that such a penalty can only infer that one is a Communist for failure to answer. Said Douglas, "The fitness of a teacher for her job turns on her devotion to that priesthood, her education, and her performance in the library, in the laboratory, and the classroom, not on her political beliefs *(17)*.

Case 4: Barenblatt v. United States (1959). The Supreme Court affirmed in 1959 in *Barenblatt v. United States (18)* that Congress has the authority to investigate, even in the field of education. The case grew out of Barenblatt's refusal to answer certain questions before the Subcommittee of the House Committee on Un-American Activities. The subcommittee was conducting an inquiry about alleged Communistic infiltration in education. Barenblatt, once a graduate assistant at the University of Michigan and later an instructor in psychology at Vassar, objected on First Amendment grounds to the subcommittee's inquiry into his beliefs and associations. When the Supreme Court heard the case after having previously remanded it, the justices split 5-4 in upholding Barenblatt's conviction.

Justice Harlan, in speaking for the majority, indicated that the case did not involve questioning into the content of academic instruction. He recognized the significance of academic freedom when he stated at the outset:

> Of course, broadly viewed, inquiries cannot be made into the teaching
> that is pursued in any of our educational institutions. When academic
> teaching—freedom and its corollary learning—freedom, so essential to the
> well-being of the Nation, are claimed, this Court will always be on the
> alert against intrusion by Congress into the constitutionally protected
> domain. But this does not mean that the Congress is precluded from in-
> terrogating a witness merely because he is a teacher. An educational
> institution is not a constitutional sanctuary from inquiries into matters
> that may otherwise be within the constitutional legislative domain merely
> for the reason that inquiry is made of someone within its walls *(19)*.

Before he dealt with the particularities of the case, Harlan emphasized the Court's recognition of the authority of Congress to enact legislation to deal with the threat of Communism. He also recognized a need for Congress to conduct inquiries preliminary to the passage of such acts. The investigative power of the Congress was extended to education when the majority said, "We think that investigatory power in this domain is not to be denied Congress solely because the field of education is involved *(20)*."

Harlan's opinion dealt with the legitimacy of the inquiry, not with the constitutionality of statutes. The Court overruled Barenblatt's claims that the subcommittee attempted to coerce him unnecessarily, expose him unfavorably, or quiz him indiscriminately. It was in this context that the Court sustained the subcommittee's authority to compel Barenblatt to testify. The Court thus held that, in this case, investigations of teachers and students about Communist associations serves the public interest far more than it infringes on one's personal liberties.

The leading dissenting opinion in *Barenblatt,* written by Justice Black and joined by Chief Justice Warren and Justice Douglas, was based on broad First Amendment grounds. Black's argument was directly opposite that of Harlan's. Black protested the Court's balancing an individual's rights with the nation's security. He rested his case on the absolute terms of the First Amendment and asserted the importance of political discussion and association. His dissent condemned the inquiry as abridging the freedom of the First Amendment by exposing the witness to scorn.

Justice Brennan's dissent contended that the investigation was conducted solely for the sake of exposing Barenblatt. Since the four dissenting justices are the same ones for whom Chief Justice Warren spoke in the *Sweezy* case, one may assume that they agree with the first quotation above by Harlan. *Barenblatt* demonstrates that, as of 1959, all nine justices of the Supreme Court had expressly recognized academic freedom as being within the area of constitutional protection.

Murphy says that:

> What a teacher says and writes, therefore, is also constitutionally protected, even though the views expressed may be "unorthodox" or "dissident" or "unpopular." That such views are protected by the first amendment the Supreme Court has said time and time again. The only novelty here is the suggestion that this may still be true when such views are held or expressed by teachers.
>
> The requirement of relevance to fitness excludes from the state's legitimate interest, and leaves within the teacher's right, associations and speech and publication which are not related to his fitness but are merely unpopular, unorthodox, or controversial (21).

Case 5: Shelton v. Tucker (1960). One year later the Court rendered another decision involving a teacher's association. *Shelton v. Tucker* (22) arose from an Arkansas statute of 1958 that required all teachers in state-supported schools and colleges to disclose the names of all organizations to which they had belonged or contributed within the preceding five years. A form was to be filled out annually.

The legislature gave as its purpose in enacting the law:

> It is hereby determined that the decisions of the United States Supreme Court in the school segregation cases require solution of a great variety of local public school problems of considerable complexity immediately and which involve the health, safety and general welfare of the people of the State of Arkansas, and that the purpose of this act is to assist in the solution of these problems and to provide for the more efficient administration of public education (23).

If the act were passed to deal with problems of integration, the Supreme Court paid scant attention to that purpose, a reference being made only in a footnote. The Court did not rest its case on the fact that membership was proscribed in the National Association for the Advancement of Colored People.

In Arkansas teachers are protected neither by civil service nor job security, as employment is on a year-to-year basis. Contracts are automatically renewed unless notice is given within ten days at the end of the school year. Shelton had taught in the public schools of Little Rock for twenty-five years. He refused to fill out the required affidavit in 1959, and his contract was not renewed for the following year.

In the meantime Shelton testified that he was not a Communist nor did he belong to any subversive organization advocating the overthrow of the government by violence. He did reveal that he was a member of the National Association for the Advancement of Colored People.

The State Supreme Court upheld the constitutionality of the Arkansas statute under which Shelton was dismissed. Appeal was then made to the United States Supreme Court.

In the nation's Supreme Court, the justices dealt first with two principles. They reiterated that a state may investigate the competence of the persons engaged to teach in the schools. They held that when a state requires a teacher to disclose all his associations, it restricts the teacher's right of association, a right closely identifiable with freedom of speech. To be decided was whether the Arkansas statute was in harmony with the first principle or whether it contravened the second. The justices in the majority agreed that there is no constitutional requirement that a teacher's classroom conduct be the sole basis for determining fitness. They held that the statute was a deprivation of a teacher's right to associational and academic liberty protected by the due process clause of the Fourteenth Amendment. Justice Stewart, in speaking for the majority, held that the state may require the disclosure of some associations but not every one, because for a teacher to be required to reveal every association is an impairment of his right of free association, closely allied with free speech. Stewart stated that when a teacher serves at the will of those to whom the disclosure is made, the situation is more alarming. He added:

> The unlimited and indiscriminate sweep of the statute now before us brings it within the ban of our prior cases. The statute's comprehensive interference with associational freedom goes far beyond what might be justified in the exercise of the State's legitimate inquiry into the fitness and competency of its teachers (24).

The majority were puzzled by the intent of the law requiring all disclosures of associations. The justices recognized that some associations have no relationship to a teacher's fitness. Stewart explained this in saying:

> The statute requires a teacher to reveal the church to which he belongs, or to which he has given financial support. It requires him to disclose his political party, and every political organization to which he may have contributed over a five-year period. It requires him to list, without number, every conceivable kind of associational tie—social, professional, political, avocational, or religious. Many such relationships could have no possible bearing upon the teacher's occupational competence or fitness (25).

Stewart asserted that teachers need to associate, that only in freedom can a teacher do his best work. He observed that the law was too damaging in how it could be used. He wrote thus:

> The statute does not provide that the information it requires be kept confidential. Each school board is left free to deal with the information

ACADEMIC FREEDOM

> as it wishes. The record contains evidence to indicate that fear of public disclosure is neither theoretical nor groundless. Even if there were no disclosure to the general public, the pressure upon a teacher to avoid any ties which might displease those who control his professional destiny would be constant and heavy. Public exposure, bringing with it the possibility of public pressures upon school boards to discharge teachers who belong to unpopular or minority organizations, would simply operate to widen and aggravate the impairment of constitutional liberty.
>
> The vigilant protection of constitutional freedoms is nowhere more vital than in the community of American schools *(26)*.

This inquiry was so indiscriminate, the majority held, that it constituted a prior restraint on the exercise of constitutionally guaranteed First Amendment freedoms, incorporated into the Fourteenth.

Kauper says that:

> ... there is a right of privacy in regard to a person's organizational activities, and that whatever power a state has to compel disclosure of its employees in regard to legitimate public interests cannot justify a statute as sweeping in its character as this statute—one which would require a person to disclose not only affiliation with organizations designed to influence public opinion and participate in the political process to improve the status of the members but affiliation also with church organizations and the like. In other words the statute was much too broad. The Court's opinion does not suggest that a more narrowly drafted statute might properly serve the state's aim. A school board might have an interest in inquiring into its teachers' outside activities in order to see to what extent teachers are spending their time on outside organizational work. But certainly any such limited and modest interests the state may properly assert would be satisfied by a much less sweeping requirement than that a complete disclosure be made of all organizations to which a member belongs or which he supports *(27)*.

Thus, a state's legitimate inquiry into the fitness and competence of its teachers must be achieved by means that are structured specifically for the objective sought rather than by techniques that stifle fundamental personal liberties.

The dissenting justices—Frankfurter, Harlan, Clark, and Whittaker —agreed that the statute was valid on its face. They saw a relationship between required disclosure and a government interest justifying it. They felt that if the information were used to fire a teacher solely for membership in an unpopular organization, then it would be a violation of due process. However, they were not ready to condemn the statute when it had not yet been abused. They held that selecting teachers according to standards is constitutionally permissible; using discriminating standards is not permissible.

Harlan's balance of interest doctrine in *Barenblatt* became the minority opinion here. He elaborated in *Shelton:*

> The rights of free speech and association embodied in the "liberty" assured against state action by the Fourteenth Amendment . . . are not absolute. . . . Where official action is claimed to invade these rights, the controlling inquiry is whether such action is justifiable on the basis as a superior governmental interest to which such individual rights must yield. When the action complained of pertains to the realm of investigation, our inquiry has a double aspect: first, whether the investigation relates to a legitimate governmental purpose; second, whether, judged in the light of that purpose, the questioned action has substantial relevance thereto. . . .
>
> It is surely indisputable that a State has the right to choose its teachers on the basis of fitness. And I think it equally clear, as the Court appears to recognize, that information about a teacher's associations may be useful to school authorities in determining the moral, professional, and social qualifications of the teacher, as well as in determining the type of service for which he will be best suited in the educational system *(28)*.

Case 6: Pickering v. Board (1968). Closely allied with the freedom of association cases is one that the Supreme Court has ruled upon which involves freedom of speech. Unlike *Sweezy* which concerned, in part, what a teacher said in a classroom, *Pickering (29)* challenged an attempt to dismiss a teacher for making damaging statements about the local board of education.

The case originated in Will County, Illinois. Marvin Pickering, a teacher in the local school system, was critical of the local board of education and its efforts to raise money through a bond issue. Pickering wrote a letter to the editor of the local newspaper in which he made statements, some false, about the board. He claimed protection under the First and Fourteenth Amendments.

Facts of the case were not in dispute. Between 1961 and 1964 four elections were held which provided for increased financial support for the schools in the county. Three elections were defeated; the second one providing for $5,500,000 to build two new schools carried.

Litigation was initiated following the fourth bond proposal, the second to be offered to the voters in 1964. Pickering, in writing the letter to the editor, criticized the manner in which the school board handled the first two elections, attacked the school board for the allocation of funds to the educational and athletic programs, and criticized the superintendent for allegedly influencing teachers not to participate in the bond election.

The school board dismissed Pickering. At the hearing required by law, the board charged that (1) Pickering's letter contained false statements, (2) publication of the letter impugned the motives of the administration, and (3) false statements damaged the school system.

Justice Marshall, speaking for the Court, held that the teacher's action was protected by the First Amendment. Justice White concurred in part and dissented in part.

ACADEMIC FREEDOM							133

Marshall rejected the notion that the school system had been harmed because of Pickering's statements. Rather, the Court held that the teacher's position reflected merely a difference of opinion and cited that the letter had appeared after the defeat of the bond issue in question. The justices supported teachers who speak out by declaring:

> Teachers are, as a class, the members of a community most likely to have informed and definite opinions as to how funds allotted to the operation of the schools should be spent. Accordingly, it is essential that they be able to speak out freely on such questions without fear of retaliatory dismissal *(30)*.

Errors in the letter related to the amount of money spent on athletics. The Court pointed out that such expenditures are a matter of public record and could easily have been corrected.

> The public interest in having free and unhindered debate on matters of public importance—the core value of the Free Speech Clause of the First Amendment—is so great that it has been held that a State cannot authorize the recovery of damages by a public official for defamatory statements directed at him except when such statements are shown to have been made either with knowledge of their falsity or with reckless disregard for their truth or falsity *(31)*.

Marshall reiterated that the Court has held that statements made by public officials on topics of public concern must be granted protection under the First Amendment, even if the statements are directed at one's superiors. He recognized that threatened dismissal can be a severe curb to free speech.

In concurring, Justice White agreed with the other justices that a school board cannot dismiss a teacher for making truthful statements innocently or negligently. He dissented in that the Court did not need to open the question of whether the statements were injurious to the school system. He would also have refrained from making an initial determination of whether Pickering knowingly published false statements.

Case 7: Ferrell v. Dallas School District (1968). Without actually rendering a decision, the Supreme Court denied certiorari in *Ferrell (32)*, an attempt to get the Court to uphold the right of a person to wear his hair any length desired. The case was on appeal from the Fifth Circuit in Texas. Having received adverse rulings, petitioners, representing a high school boy, sought relief in the Supreme Court. Justice Douglas would have heard the case and stated so in a three-paragraph dissent. He said:

> It comes as a surprise that in a country where the States are restrained by an Equal Protection Clause, a person can be denied edu-

cation in a public school because of the length of his hair. I suppose that a nation bent on turning out robots might insist that every male have a crew cut and every female wear pigtails. But the ideas of "life, liberty and the pursuit of happiness" expressed in the Declaration of Independence, later found specific definition in the Constitution itself, including of course freedom of expression and a wide zone of privacy. I had supposed those guarantees permitted idiosyncrasies to flourish, especially when they concern the image of one's personality and his philosophy toward government and his fellow men.

Municipalities furnish many services to their inhabitants; and I had supposed that it would be an invidious discrimination to withhold fire protection, police protection, garbage collection, health protection, and the like merely because a person was an offbeat nonconformist when it came to hairdo and dress as well as to diet, race, religion, or his views on Vietnam (33).

Case 8: Tinker v. Des Moines School District (1969). The *Tinker* case (34) is the only decision of the United States Supreme Court during the Warren regime to treat freedom of speech of students. It grew out of an attempt by school officials to curb student protest of the Vietnam War. The Court upheld the right of students to protest, but it did not sanction all kinds and degrees of protest.

Five opinions were handed down. Justice Fortas wrote the majority opinion, and Justices White and Stewart concurred in separate opinions. Separate dissenting opinions were registered by Justices Harlan and Black.

The case began in December 1965 when a group of students decided to protest the Vietnam War by wearing black armbands during the holiday season and by fasting on December 16 and December 31. Aware of the students' plans, school principals adopted a policy covering the wearing of armbands. Any student so attired would be asked to remove the armband; failure to comply would result in suspension. Petitioners were aware of the regulation.

On December 16 two students, Mary Beth Tinker, aged fifteen, and Christopher Eckhardt, aged sixteen, wore the bands to school. The following day Mary Beth's brother, John, aged fifteen, wore a black armband also. All three students were suspended and did not return to school until after New Year's Day. An injunction was sought to restrain school officials from disciplining the students, and parents sought to recover nominal damages.

The majority of the Court asserted that:

> First Amendment rights, applied in light of the special characteristics of the school environment, are available to teachers and students. It can hardly be argued that either students or teachers shed their constitutional rights to freedom of speech or expression at the schoolhouse gate. This has been the unmistakable holding of this Court for almost 50 years (35).

Fortas cited the problem in this case: balancing First Amendment rights with rules of school authorities. Unlike some kinds of student expressions such as hair styles or length of skirts, the immediate case involved a fundamental right of the First Amendment—freedom of speech. The majority recognized that there was no evidence of noisy or disruptive demonstrations; neither was there any indication of the students' interfering with normal school routine or with the rights of other students. The only undesirable activity transpired outside class when a few students made hostile remarks to the armband-clad pupils. The record showed that of the 18,000 students in the school system, seven children had worn armbands, and five had been suspended.

The district court had upheld the action of school authorities who had expressed fear that violence might occur. In answer to this position the Supreme Court answered:

> In order for the State in the person of school officials to justify prohibition of a particular expression of opinion, it must be able to show that its action was caused by something more than a mere desire to avoid the discomfort and unpleasantness that always accompany an unpopular viewpoint (36).

It was pointed out that an official memorandum by school officials after the incident gave no indication of anticipated disruption. The Court suggested that school officials may have been wanting to avoid controversy, for recently a student had been dissuaded from writing an article about the Vietnam War for the school newspaper. An inconsistency was pointed out in school authorities' permitting students to wear political buttons, including an Iron Cross.

Fortas continued:

> In our system, state-operated schools may not be enclaves of totalitarianism. School officials do not possess absolute authority over their students. Students in school as well as out of school are "persons" under our Constitution. They are possessed of fundamental rights which the State must respect, just as they themselves must respect their obligations to the State. . . . In the absence of a specific showing of constitutionally valid reasons to regulate their speech, students are entitled to freedom of expression of their views (37).

Fortas held further that this case is not confined to what transpires in the classroom; rather, the principle extends to cover various kinds of activities in various places, including the cafeteria and playground.

The Court did not consider the matter of relief for damages.

Stewart concurred, while holding that First Amendment rights for adults and children differ. In White's concurring opinion he noted that the Court continued to recognize a difference in communicating by words and by acts.

In his dissent, Justice Harlan recognized that school officials are not exempt from the Fourteenth Amendment, but he would give officials considerable latitude in maintaining discipline in the schools.

Justice Black was very outspoken in denouncing the majority opinion. He opened his dissent:

> The Court's holding in this case ushers in what I deem to be an entirely new era in which the power to control pupils by the elected "officials of state supported public schools . . ." in the United States is in ultimate effect transferred to the Supreme Court *(38)*.

Black held that the majority based their holding on two propositions: (1) The wearing of armbands is symbolic speech. (2) Public schools can accommodate symbolic speech so long as there are no disruptions. The justice then stated:

> While I have always believed that under the First and Fourteenth Amendments neither the State nor Federal Government has any authority to regulate or censor the content of speech, I have never believed that any person has a right to give speeches or engage in demonstrations where he pleases and when he pleases *(39)*.

Black concluded his dissent by speaking philosophically:

> Change has been said to be truly the law of life but sometimes the old and the tried and true are worth holding. The schools of this Nation have undoubtedly contributed to giving us tranquility and to making us a more law-abiding people. Uncontrolled and uncontrolable liberty is an enemy to domestic peace. We cannot close our eyes to the fact that some of the country's greatest problems are crimes committed by the youth, too many of school age. School discipline, like parental discipline, is an integral and important part of training our children to be good citizens —to be better citizens. Here a very small number of students have crisply and summarily refused to obey a school order designed to give pupils who want to learn the opportunity to do so. One does not need to be a prophet to know that after the Court's holding today that some students in Iowa schools and indeed in all schools will be ready, able, and willing to defy their teachers on practically all orders. This is the more unfortunate for the schools since groups of students all over the land are already running loose, conducting break-ins, sit-ins, lie-ins, and smash-ins. . . . Students engaged in such activities are apparently confident that they know far more about how to operate public school systems than do their parents, teachers, and elected school officials. . . . Turned loose with law suits for damages and injunctions against their teachers like they are here, it is nothing but wishful thinking to image that young, immature students will not soon believe it is their right to control the schools rather than the right of the States that collect the taxes to hire the teachers for the benefit of the pupils. This case, therefore, wholly without constitutional reasons in my judgment, subjects all the public schools in the country to the whims and caprices of their loudest-mouth-

ed, but maybe not their brightest students. . . . I wish, therefore, wholly to disclaim any purpose on my part, to hold that the Federal Constitution compels the teachers, parents, and elected school officials to surrender control of the American public school system to public school students *(40).*

Because *Tinker* is the only case involving freedom of speech for students, because of the lack of agreement of the justices, and because it is unrelated to the association cases involving teachers, it is reviewed without being analyzed.

Common Elements of the Cases

Investigation of past activities. The cases just reviewed dealt with the teacher's past associations. In the *Slochower* case, the inquiry extended back as far as twelve years, and *Beilan* concerned a teacher's associations eight years previous to the interrogation. Both *Sweezy* and *Barenblatt* dealt with past associations, although the specific time lapse between the association in question and the inquiry was not cited. *Shelton* differed from the other four cases in that this one was based on the written record covering a teacher's associations for the last five years. In all of these cases, however, it was the teacher's past, not the present association, under question.

Screening of teachers. Beilan is the controlling case involving the screening of teachers. Both *Barenblatt* and *Shelton* relied on it. Moreover, *Beilan's* decision rested on *Adler,* which the Court cited in *Slochower, Beilan, Barenblatt,* and *Shelton.* The Court held in *Beilan* that asking a teacher about association or affiliation with the Communist Party was relevant to the state's interest in an employee. Refusal to answer amounted to statutory incompetency. In questions about his associations, a teacher must therefore be forthright in answering his superintendent.

Shelton differed from *Beilan* in that the investigation was too sweeping. This case also held that information about teachers could potentially be misused.

The Court held in *Sweezy* that an investigation of a teacher could not impinge on that persons's First Amendment freedoms, namely freedom of political expression and association. *Slochower* held that an investigation must be consistent with the state's interests. Fitness for teaching was not directly related to the *Barenblatt* inquiry.

Nature of association. Subversive activities was the subject matter of four of the five cases. Of these four, *Slochower, Beilan,* and *Barenblatt* concerned the teacher's relationship with the Communist Party.

Sweezy dealt with an investigation of the petitioner's affiliation with the Progressive and Communist Parties. *Shelton* did not deal with subversion; rather, it was concerned with a state's attempt to regulate membership in organizations generally.

Pertinence of the inquiry. The Court recognized that investigation into a teacher's suitability for the classroom turned on many factors. Said the Court in *Beilan*, "We find no requirement in the Federal Constitution that a teacher's classroom conduct be the sole basis for determining his fitness. Fitness for teaching depends on a broad range of factors *(41)*." The questions asked of the petitioner were held to be relevant.

A standard was set up in *Shelton*. There the Court held that a state may require a teacher to reveal his associational ties, but to ask that all be revealed is too sweeping and, therefore, unconstitutional. This case cited the quotation above from *Beilan* as precedent.

Another standard for an inquiry was made in *Slochower*. There the Court ruled that an investigation by a Senate investigating committee was not related to the city's interest. It would hold, therefore, that a teacher's dismissal based on a non-school inquiry must be predicated on an investigation related to the affairs of the state or its subsidiary. *Sweezy* held that there was no connection in the questioning of the petitioner with the interest of the state. *Barenblatt* recognized the authority of Congress to investigate in the field of education, but it did not reveal any standard.

Cooperation with investigating officials. Each of the persons engaged in education refused to give requested or required information prior to court action's being initiated. The Fifth Amendment was specifically invoked by Slochower before a congressional committee while, before a similar committee, Barenblatt refused to answer, although he did not plead the Fifth Amendment. Sweezy and Beilan declined to answer, respectively, the attorney general and the superintendent. Shelton failed to complete a written form on request.

Dismissal action. The teachers involved, except Barenblatt, were dismissed for refusing to cooperate with the investigating officials. Dismissal was not a factor in *Barenblatt*. Both Beilan and Shelton were fired for not supplying school officials with requested information. Beilan refused to answer the superintendent's questions while Shelton declined to complete the school form based upon a state statute. With the other two teachers, the dismissal followed an insistence on not answering investigating officials—with Sweezy, the attorney general; with Slochower, a Senate investigating committee. In *Pickering* the teacher was dismissed, not so much for failure to cooperate as for being outspoken against the administration.

Constitutional protection. The due process clause of the Fourteenth Amendment controlled four of the eight cases. *Slochower, Beilan,* and *Shelton* relied exclusively on it. Sweezy used that clause as well as sought protection under the First Amendment. The Supreme Court, however, recognized the due process clause as controlling the case. Barenblatt pleaded protection under the First Amendment; however, the Court also relied on the Fourteenth for its decision. *Pickering* was controlled by the First Amendment.

Extent of investigation. These cases have brought the authority of investigation of teachers under local, state, and federal officials. Before *Barenblatt,* investigation did not extend beyond the state. The extension of inquiry into education to the federal level is the guiding principle in *Barenblatt.*

The Cases Involving Loyalty Oaths

For a number of years employees, as a condition of engaging in certain occupations, have been required to take loyalty oaths. Over half of the states require a school teacher to sign an oath stating that he will support the Constitution and defend the country against all enemies. The oath has little impact on teachers except to annoy some who do not feel the need of being singled out for this sort of thing. Those adopting and administering the oath, however, feel that a teacher owes his loyalty to the public; taking the oath affirms that expression of allegiance.

Loyalty oaths that have provoked opposition and have been challenged are different from those stated above. More recent oath laws have resulted, in part, from a concern over the spread of Communism and other subversive organizations and influences. Bryson indicated in a 1961 study that:

> Seven states and the District of Columbia have loyalty oath provisions requiring teachers to swear or affirm that they have no membership in the Communist Party. Six states and the District of Columbia have loyalty oath prescriptions requiring teachers to swear or affirm that they do not hold membership in either subversive organizations or the Communist Party *(42).*

The newer oaths are designed to reveal past loyalty or disloyalty. They are negatively structured, asking that the person taking them state that he has not done or will refrain from doing a certain thing, particularly hold membership in the Communist Party or other subversive organizations. The oath laws are designed to prevent or to terminate the employment of persons failing to meet the test of the law.

The oath laws may vary in form. They may require a sworn statement that one is not a member of the Communist Party. They may require that one swear that he is not and has not been a member of an organization listed by school authorities or state officials as being subversive.

Refusal to take the oath usually results in a teacher's dismissal. Some teachers have objected to compliance, not because of disloyalty, but because of resentment against the oath requirement istself. Others cite the peril and the potential misuse of the requirement. May one have held membership in the Communist Party only to resign when he became aware of the real nature of the party? Should one be penalized without a hearing for membership in an organization on an attorney general's list? May nominal membership be held wherein no harmful activity is plotted?

The Supreme Court heard five cases during the time Warren was Chief Justice which dealt directly with the loyalty oath in the public schools. The five were attacked as being in violation of the Fourteenth Amendment. The Court overturned each statute.

Case 1: Cramp v. Board (1961). In *Cramp v. Board of Public Instruction of Orange County (43),* the Court invalidated an oath for a public employee which required him not only to deny membership in the Communist Party but also to swear, "that I have not and will not lend my aid, support, advice, counsel, or influence to the Communist Party. . . ." Cramp had taught for nine years in Orange County before it was discovered that he had not taken the oath. Upon being requested to comply with the requirement, he refused. He then sought an injunction to prevent his being forced to take the oath and to prevent his discharge for not taking it. He also sought to declare the law unconstitutional.

Testimony in the Circuit Court revealed that Cramp:

> has, does and will support the Constitution of the United States and of the State of Florida; he is not a member of the Communist Party; that he has not, does not and will not lend aid, support, advice, counsel or influence to the Communist Party; he does not believe in the overthrow of the United States or of the State of Florida by force or violence; he is not a member of any organization or party which believes in or teaches directly or indirectly the overthrow of the Government of the United States or of Florida by force or violence *(44).*

The United States Supreme Court was asked to decide if Florida could force an employee to take an oath, at the risk of prosecution or

ACADEMIC FREEDOM 141

perjury, or face dismissal. Justice Stewart, in writing the Court's opinion, made note of the omissions in the act:

> The provision of the oath here in question, it is to be noted, says nothing of advocacy of violent overthrow of state or federal government. It says nothing of membership or affiliation with the Communist Party, past or present. The provision is completely lacking in these or any other terms susceptible of objective measurement (45).

The Court was unable to determine what the statute meant by the terms "aid, support, advice, counsel, or influence." Stewart noted that candidates for the Communist Party have been on the ballot in many states and that the party has endorsed others for office. He wondered if, under the act in question, lawyers could represent a member of the Communist Party.

In overturning the act for its ambiguity, the Court said:

> a statute which either forbids or requires the doing of an act in terms so vague that men of common intelligence must necessarily guess at its meaning and differ as to its application, violates the first essential of due process of law (46).

The Court held that, to sustain constitutionality, oaths must pass a test of objective measurement. An indefinite, vague oath the justices held, may create two evils. It may restrain an individual's freedom by having him speak at his own risk, curtailing the amount of free speech and consequently diminishing the free dissemination of ideas. The second evil is a burden of speculation one must attach to the oath's meaning. An oath law may be so vague that no real standard can be applied to it. Morris states that:

> Due process of law requires that a man be given clear notice of that speech and those associations which have been prohibited; and stricter standards of clarity apply to laws which have a potentially deterring impact on freedom of speech (47).

Cramp does not show what the standard is or should be. It shows what it is not. In commenting about vague standards, Rice says:

> one might be discouraged by such an oath requirement from joining the American Civil Liberties Union which has lent its "advice" and "counsel" to persons accused of Communist Party membership in cases involving what the Union considers important civil liberties. However, the Florida court had ruled that "the element of scienter" was implicit in each of the requirements of the statute. Perhaps if the Florida court had particularized this requirement of scienter, so that the employee must have rendered the assistance to the Party in order specifically and willfully to promote its unlawful purposes and not for any innocent purpose such as the protection of constitutional rights by provision of legal counsel to accused Party members, the oath provision might have been

saved. The *Cramp* case illustrates the incongruity of treating the Party as a criminal conspiracy for some purposes and as a valid political association for others. Such ambivalence accentuates the uncertainty of the extent to which one may deal with the Party while at the same time it fails to extirpate the Communist conspiracy *(48)*.

Case 2. Baggett v. Bullitt (1964). Baggett v. Bullitt *(49)* also involved a loyalty oath for teachers. The case was filed under a claim that a 1955 law of the state of Washington was unduly vague. All state employees, including teachers, were required to execute this 1931 oath:

> I solemnly swear (or affirm) that I will support the constitution and laws of the United States of America and of the State of Washington, and will by precept and example promote respect for the flag and the institutions of the United States of America and the State of Washington, reverence for law and order and undivided allegiance to the government of the United States *(50)*.

The 1955 statute provided that employment would be denied to any subversive person. The statute described such a person thus:

> "Subversive person" means any person who commits, attempts to commit, or aids in the commission, or advocates, abets, advises or teaches by any means any person to commit, attempt to commit, or aid in the commission of any act intended to overthrow, destroy, or alter, or to assist in the overthrow, destruction or alteration of, the constitutional form of the government of the United States, or of the state of Washington, or any political subdivision of either of them by revolution, force, or violence *(51)*. . . .

The act declared the Communist Party as being a subversive organization and membership in it as being a subversive activity. The act was challenged by sixty-four members of the faculty, staff, and students at the University of Washington. The Supreme Court relied on *Cramp* for precedent. It confined its decision to a consideration of the statute as being vague, uncertain, and broad. Justice White wrote the majority opinion, viewing the teacher's obligation to follow the oath, even though vague:

> Those with a conscientious regard for what they solemnly swear or affirm, sensitive to the perils posed by the oath's indefinite language, avoid the risk of loss of employment, and perhaps profession, only by restricting their conduct to that which is unquestionably safe. Free speech may not be so inhibited *(52)*.
>
> Well-intentioned prosecutors and judicial safeguards do not neutralize the vice of a vague law. Nor should we encourage the casual taking of oaths by upholding the discharge or exclusion from public employment of those with a conscientious and scrupulous regard for such undertaking *(53)*.

> The State may not require one to choose between subscribing to an unduly vague and broad oath, thereby incurring the likelihood of prosecution, and conscientiously refusing to take the oath with the consequent loss of employment, and perhaps profession, particularly where "the free dissemination of ideas may be the loser" *(54)*.

The Court's decision in *Baggett* rested on the argument wherein *Cramp* was decided. This indefinite, vague oath law reached beyond constitutional limits by subjecting teachers to the peril of guessing when the statute might be violated.

Case 3: Elfbrandt v. *Russell (1966) (55)*. The third case involving loyalty oaths grew out of an Arizona statute requiring state employees to subscribe to the following oath:

> I, (type or print name) do solemnly swear (or affirm) that I will support the Constitution of the United States and the Constitution and laws of the State of Arizona; that I will bear true faith and allegiance to the same, and defend them against all enemies, foreign and domestic, and that I will faithfully and impartially discharge the duties of the office of (name of office) according to the best of my ability, so help me God (or so I do affirm) *(56)*.

The state legislature made as subject for prosecution for perjury and termination of employment anyone taking the oath who "knowingly and wilfully becomes a member of the communist [sic] party of the United States or its successors or any of its subordinate organizations or any other organization having for one of its purposes the overthrow of the government of Arizona or any of its political subdivisions where the employee had knowledge of the unlawful purpose *(57)*."

Elfbrandt, a teacher in the public schools, refused to take the oath, not knowing what it meant and not being able to have a hearing to have the statute clarified. Litigation followed. The United States Supreme Court vacated the judgment of the Arizona Supreme Court and remanded the case for further consideration in light of *Baggett* v. *Bullitt*. Before the nation's highest court the second time, the oath law was overturned by the justices in a 5-4 decision. Justice Douglas wrote the majority opinion in which Justices Warren, Black, Brennan, and Fortas concurred. Justice White dissented and was joined in his opinion by Justices Clark, Harlan, and Stewart.

In the majority opinion Justice Douglas relied on *Baggett* v. *Bullitt* plus non-school cases to support his position. He noted that "membership clause" cases previously had been upheld because they involved only active membership specifically intended to promote the overthrow of the government or the organization's unlawful ends. Douglas concluded, "nothing in the oath, the statutory gloss, or the construction of the oath and statutes given by the Arizona Supreme Court, purports to exclude association by one who does not subscribe to the organization's unlawful ends *(58)*." Justice Douglas then posed the questions about one's possible affiliations. He answered, "Those who join an organization but do not share its unlawful purposes and who do not participate in its unlawful activities surely pose no threat, either as citizens or as public employees *(59)*."

The justices in the majority reaffirmed that loyalty oath laws must be written clearly and narrowly so as to describe and punish specific conduct as an unquestioned danger to the state. The Arizona law failed to meet this standard.

The dissenting justices held to the position that a state may condition public employment upon persons "abstaining from knowing membership in the Communist Party and other organizations advocating the violent overthrow of the government which employs them; the state is constitutionally authorized to inquire into such affiliations and it may discharge those who refuse to affirm or deny them *(60)*." After citing eight cases, Justice White noted that the majority did not mention or overrule these cases. The dissenting justices held that the statute was too broad in that it included employees who are knowing members but who may be inactive and who may have no intention of furthering the illegal aims of the Communist Party.

Case 4: Whitehall v. Elkins (1967). The fourth case to be heard by the Warren Court challenging loyalty oath laws for public school personnel was *Whitehall v. Elkins (61).*

The oath law was contested by Howard Joseph Whitehall, who had been offered a teaching position at the University of Maryland. It stated as follows:

> I, ————, do hereby (Print Name—including middle initial) certify that I am not engaged in one way or another in the attempt to overthrow the Government of the United States, or the State of Maryland, or any political subdivision of either of them, by force or violence *(62).*

Implementing the oath law was the Ober Act, which defined a subversive person and a subversive organization. The Supreme Court was called upon to rule on the legality of the oath law and sections 1 and 13 of the Ober Act.

Justice Douglas, speaking for the Court and basing the decision on the First Amendment, overturned the oath requirements. In condemning the oath, Douglas stated that "The continuing surveillance which this type of law places on teachers is hostile to academic freedom *(63)*." He

ACADEMIC FREEDOM   145

added, "The lines between permissible and impermissible conduct are quite indistinct. Precision and clarity are not present *(64)*."

Justices Harlan, Stewart, and White dissented, contending that the oath law was designed only for one to disclaim actual present activity. The justices in the minority would look no further. In refuting the majority's position, Harlan, speaking for the minority, stated, "The only thing that does shine through the opinion of the majority is that its members do not like loyalty oaths *(65)*."

Case 5: Keyishian v. Board of Regents (1967). The Warren Court handed down its fifth and final loyalty oath decision in *Keyishian (66)*, a challenge to the Feinberg Law of New York.

Four members of the faculty of the University of Buffalo, a division of the State University of New York, refused to reveal if they had ever been Communists, a statement that was to be transmitted to the President of the State University. A fifth appellant, a part-time lecturer in English and a non-faculty library employee, was not required to sign the oath, but refused to answer if he had been a Communist. He was dismissed.

The case hinged on two laws of New York: the Civil Service Law and the Feinberg Law, a supplement to the state's education law. The appellants attacked three sections of the Civil Service Law: (1) No person was to be employed by the state who (a) advocated overthrow of the government by force, violence, or other unlawful means, (b) prepared or distributed any material advocating overthrow, or (c) organized or became a member of a party advocating overthrow. (2) A person declared ineligible or dismissed might petition for a hearing. (3) A person uttering treasonable or seditious words or committing treasonable or seditious acts would be discharged.

The appellants also charged that two sections of the education laws were unconstitutional. One provision in question (section 3021) empowered school authorities to remove employees for treasonable or seditious acts or utterances. Section 3022 authorized the Board of Regents to make and enforce rules for the removal of persons deemed unfit to teach. The Board was also instructed to prepare a list, subject to periodic revision, of subversive organizations. Membership in a listed organization would constitute *prima facie* evidence of disqualification. Further, Regents were to make an annual report to the legislature.

Before the Supreme Court in 1952, the Feinberg Law had been upheld in *Adler.* A year later New York extended the law to cover personnel in institutions of higher learning, and the same year the Communist Party was listed as being subversive. In 1956 the Board of

Regents required that applicants sign the "Feinberg Certificate"—an explanation to the President of the University of any Communist Party affiliation. The appellants refused to comply.

In 1965 the "Feinberg Certificate" requirement was rescinded and supplanted by the following pronouncements:

1. Sections 3021 and 3022 will be a part of one's contract.
2. A person will be informed of his disqualification stemming from membership in a subversive organization.
3. A personal interview will be granted any person requesting it.
4. If an applicant refuses to answer any relevant question he will not be recommended for employment.
5. A brochure explaining the legal effect of the statutes will be given each applicant.
6. No disclaimer oath will be required.

A 5-4 decision by the United States Supreme Court declared the statutes in question to be in violation of the freedom of association guarantee of the First Amendment. Joining Justice Brennan, author of the opinion, were Justices Warren, Black, Douglas, and Fortas. Justice Clark dissented and was joined in his opinion by Justices Harlan, Stewart, and White. The voting cleavage was the same as that in *Elfbrandt*, decided a year earlier.

The majority attacked the laws' requirements on two major grounds: vagueness and overbreadth. Brennan expressed concern over lack of clarity in the statutes with respect to the meaning of "treason" and particularly "sedition." The legislators had accepted the meaning of the two words as they appear in the penal code. Brennan indicated that since sedition is equated with criminal anarchy, it poses two hypothetical questions—(1) Does one commit a felony if he displays a book advocating overthrow of the government? (2) Does a teacher, carrying a copy of Marx on the streets, advocate criminal anarchy? Brennan stated, "We cannot gainsay the potential effect of this obscure wording on those with a conscience and scrupulous regard for such undertakings *(67)*." He then cited the potential peril to the teacher:

> The teacher cannot know the extent, if any, to which a "seditious" utterance must transcend mere statement about abstract doctrine, the extent to which it must be intended to and tend to indoctrinate or incite to action in furtherance of the defined doctrine. The crucial consideration is that no teacher can know just where the line is drawn between "seditious" and nonseditious utterances and acts *(68)*.

It was recognized that the state had an interest in wanting to protect the educational system from subversives; however, the statutes had overextended themselves by including as subversion the writing of articles, distribution of pamphlets, and endorsement of speeches. The justice continued:

> Our Nation is deeply committed to safeguarding academic freedom which is of transcendent value to all of us and not merely to the teacher concerned. That freedom is therefore a special concern of the First Amendment, which does not tolerate laws that cast a pall of orthodoxy over the classroom.
>
> The classroom is peculiarly the "marketplace of ideas." The Nation's future depends upon leaders trained through wide exposure to that robust exchange of ideas which discovers truth "out of a multitude of tongues" [rather] than through any kind of authoritative selection *(69)*.

Brennan then cited a need for allowing persons considerable latitude in exercising First Amendment freedoms if those rights are to survive. For teachers to be ineligible for service, they must be clearly informed of what is being or is not being sanctioned.

In attacking the overbreadth of the statutes, the Court indicated that, since *Adler*, a new constitutional standard had developed and was expressed by both *Elfbrandt* and *Aptheker:*

> ... legislation which sanctions membership unaccompanied by specific intent to further the unlawful goals of the organization or which is not active membership violates constitutional limitations *(70)*.

The Court thus held that the Civil Service Law and the Education Law are too broad in that they seek to bar employment for association which may be sanctioned consistent with First Amendment rights. The distinction is made between mere knowing membership without specific purpose of overthrow and membership actively engaged in unlawful overthrow.

The tone of the majority's vigorous dissent is indicated in Justice Clark's opening sentence:

> The blunderbuss fashion in which the majority couches "its artillery of words" together with the morass of cases it cites as authority and the obscurity of their application to the question at hand makes it difficult to grasp the true thrust of its decision *(71)*.

Clark proceeded to refute the majority opinion based on three contentions: (1) a moot question, (2) speculative issues, and (3) nonexhausted administrative remedies.

Although the "Feinberg Certificate" had not been applicable for two years, the Court struck it down. Section 3021, inapplicable also to appellants, was also voided. Further, that section did not apply to teachers in the state university; it covered only teachers in the public schools.

Justice Clark noted that in the past the Court had not passed on speculative issues. One of the provisions of the act was not scheduled to become effective until September 1, 1967, and no member of the educational system had been charged with violation of it. Clark observed that the Court seemed to be "building straw men."

The minority asserted that the appellants had not exhausted their administrative remedies; they had not pursued the remedy of judicial review provided by the Civil Service Law. Clark concluded that, "No Court has ever reached out so far to destroy so much with so little *(72)*."

Common Elements of the Cases

The five loyalty oath decisions have placed a burden on members of the Supreme Court to weigh the protection of society against the teacher's exercise of academic freedom. The route the Court has taken is clear: it has minimized a danger or a potential danger to the state or to the students of having subversive or potentially subversive persons in the classroom as instructors. Rather, the justices have recognized that advantages accrue from one's being exposed to many different ideas. Unlike *Adler*, recent decisions do not indicate that children are of an impressionable age, and that they may be too immature to understand and then accept or refute ideologies which may be unpopular or subversive.

Academic freedom is all-important to the teacher, and it has been granted constitutional protection. The Warren Court has reaffirmed its belief that teachers should not be overly restricted, for academic freedom would then be restricted. Possible effects of giving teachers considerable latitude in teaching and in association might be an inefficiency of the school program and a forum for the non-conformist, but the Court apparently does not see a danger in either of these.

The loyalty oath decisions do reaffirm the notion that states have a responsibility in protecting students from teachers guilty of advocating unlawful overthrow of the government. However, membership in an unpopular or even subversive organization may not be just cause for termination of a teacher's contract. Like other citizens, teachers have the right to examine or be exposed to a variety of ideas.

The Court has also recognized that the right of association of the First Amendment is basic to all teachers. Constitutional protection of this right is given without distinction to instructors in both public schools and universities.

The Court has made it very clear that in order for an oath law to be upheld, it must meet a standard of objective measurement. The fact that all five loyalty oath laws were overturned is an indication that the Court will not tolerate a negatively structured oath.

Since the loyalty oath decisions were decided on such close voting of the justices, one concludes that there is lack of substantial agreement as to the existence of a national crisis necessitating antisubversive legislation.

States may enact laws designed to protect students and preserve the schools from subversion; the Supreme Court has not prohibited this. Legislators, however, are faced with two problems. They must first ascertain what activity or association by teachers may legitimately be proscribed by a loyalty oath. They must then structure a statute of such clarity as to make the restriction readily understood. Having overturned since 1952 all six loyalty oath laws involving teachers, the Supreme Court has indicated what criteria are not constitutional. Future decisions may reveal what might meet the Court's test of legality.

Summary

The cases just treated indicate a lack of agreement among the justices as to the degree of academic freedom the Constitution gives teachers. Of the twelve major cases examined at length, six were decided by a 5-4 majority; excluding *Ferrell*, other cases had a number of dissenting opinions. In one case the Court could not get five justices to agree on the reasoning leading to the decision.

The Court has revealed through the majority opinions that the teacher's freedom may not arbitrarily be restricted. No attempt has been made by the justices to determine what the limits of freedom are that a teacher may enjoy. The decisions have dealt more with procedural rather than with substantive safeguards. This very fact limits one in analyzing common elements of these cases. A brief summary of the decision of each case follows.

Slochower v. *Board of Higher Education of New York (1956)*. A teacher cannot be automatically dismissed for invoking the Fifth Amendment. Due process is violated without a hearing being held first. One should not infer guilt from a person's refusal to testify.

Sweezy v. *New Hampshire, by Wyman, Attorney General (1957)*. An individual's rights have preferred status to legislative enactments which delegate responsibilities to the executive branch. The legislative inquiry cannot extend to what one teaches in a classroom, for it is a violation of academic freedom, closely allied with freedom of speech. An investigation about a teacher's affiliation with the Progressive Party is unconstitutional when made by a delegated agency operating under broad, unclear guidelines.

Beilan v. *Board of Public Education, School District of Philadelphia (1958).* A teacher may be discharged for incompetence for refusal to answer questions of his employer about alleged membership in subversive organizations. A superintendent may make inquiries about a teacher's out-of-class activities as a basis for determining fitness in the classroom.

Barenblatt v. *United States (1959).* Since the legislature enacts laws to deal with subversion, it may also make inquiries about subversive threats—as a basis for lawmaking. This right of inquiry extends to education.

Shelton et al. v. *Tucker et al. (1960).* School officials may require the disclosure of some associations, for classroom performance is not the sole index of fitness. However, a statute requiring the disclosure of all associations is violative of due process.

Cramp v. *Board of Public Instruction of Orange County (1961).* A statute requiring teachers to swear that they have not given "aid, support, advice, counsel, or influence" to the Communist Party is overly vague and cannot be enforced.

Baggett v. *Bullitt (1964).* A state statute requiring all teachers to take an oath and providing for the termination of employment of any teacher enrolled in a subversive organization or advocating the overthrow of the government by force or violence suffers from ambiguity.

Elfbrandt v. *Russell (1966).* A statute making as ineligible for state employment anyone who will not take a required oath and who knowingly is a member of the Communist Party or a subversive organization is unconstitutional.

Whitehall v. *Elkins (1967).* Maryland's loyalty oath law denying employment to anyone advocating overthrow of the government is unconstitutional.

Keyishian v. *Board of Regents (1967).* New York's loyalty oath law was overturned on the grounds of overbreadth and vagueness.

Pickering v. *Board (1968).* Freedom of speech of the First Amendment protects a teacher who publishes critical statements, even though they be false.

Ferrell v. *Dallas School District (1968).* School officials may require a pupil to cut his hair.

Tinker v. *Des Moines School District (1969).* Students may engage in protests at school provided such activity is not disruptive.

The Supreme Court has recognized that freedom of association is closely allied with freedom of speech of the First Amendment and reinforced by the due process clause of the Fourteenth Amendment. School officials may not deny a teacher his freedom of speech or association as a condition of employment. The Court has held consistently, however, that public employment is a privilege and cannot be guaranteed to any citizen. While it would hold that no employer may discharge a teacher for exercising his rights of free speech and association, it would also hold that a choice might conceivably have to be made between public employment and some association a teacher wishes to make, allegedly subversive.

Investigation into the extent of one's associations can be made, the Court has held, except where the individual's fundamental rights and interests are transgressed or where the inquiring officials abuse their privileges. The Constitution then serves as the protector of the teacher.

The loyalty oath cases do not state nor imply that all loyalty oath laws are invalid. Both *Cramp* and *Baggett* reveal that the Court will strike down ambiguous legislation providing for punishment of offenders. The Court has stated, moreover, that it would impose even stricter standards against vagueness that impairs individual liberties. In both of these cases, the individual liberty outweighed the state's interests of protecting itself from the threat of subversive influences.

The holdings of *Cramp* and *Baggett* indicate that a state may not terminate employment of teachers for their refusal to take an oath or because of membership in an organization covered by an oath unless the employee had knowledge of the organization's unlawful nature and purpose. A contract may not be voided, moreover, for a teacher's innocent membership in an organization proscribed by an oath. The Court has also held that an oath may violate due process by being too vague, broad, or ambiguous.

Balancing the individual's rights with the nation's interests has not been clearly settled by the Court. In several cases the Court has dealt with the problem but has not given opinions consistently favoring one concept. The Court has based its decision on the merits of each individual case.

Notes to Chapter V

1. William E. Stevenson, "Education and Freedom," *School and Society*, LXXXIV (December 22, 1956), 213.

2. Robert Hoffman, "A Note on Academic Freedom," *Phi Delta Kappan*, XLIV (January, 1963), 185.

3. *Adler et al.* v. *Board of Education of the City of New York*, 342 U.S. 485 (1952), p. 508.
4. *Slochower* v. *Board of Higher Education of New York City*, 350 U.S. 551 (1956).
5. *Ibid.*, p. 558.
6. *Ibid.*, p. 557.
7. *Ibid.*, p. 559.
8. *Sweezy* v. *New Hampshire, by Wyman, Attorney General*, 354 U.S. 234 (1957).
9. *Ibid.*, p. 245.
10. *Ibid.*, p. 250.
11. R. R. Hamilton (ed.), "Legislative Committee May Not Inquire Into Subject Matter of Teacher's Lectures," *The National School Law Reporter*, VIII (February 12, 1959), 94.
12. *Beilan* v. *Board of Public Education, School District of Philadelphia*, 357 U.S. 399 (1958).
13. Cited at *Ibid.*, p. 406.
14. *Ibid.*, pp. 405, 406.
15. *Ibid.*, p. 410.
16. *Ibid.*, p. 411.
17. *Ibid.*, p. 415.
18. *Barenblatt* v. *United States*, 360 U.S. 109 (1959).
19. *Ibid.*, p. 112.
20. *Ibid.*, p. 129.
21. William P. Murphy, "Academic Freedom—An Emerging Constitutional Right," *Law and Contemporary Problems*, XXVIII (Summer, 1963), 465.
22. *Shelton et al.* v. *Tucker et al.*, 364 U.S. 479 (1960).
23. *Ibid.*, p. 483.
24. *Ibid.*, p. 490.
25. *Ibid.*, p. 488.
26. *Ibid.*, p. 486.
27. Paul G. Kauper, *Civil Liberties and the Constitution* (Ann Arbor: The University of Michigan Press, 1962), p. 101.
28. *Shelton, op. cit.*, p. 497.
29. *Pickering* v. *Board of Education of Township High School District 205, Will County, Illinois*, 391 U.S. 563 (1968).
30. *Ibid.*, p. 572.
31. *Ibid.*, p. 573.
32. *Ferrell et al.* v. *Dallas Independent School District et al.*, 393 U.S. 856 (1968).
33. *Ibid.*
34. *Tinker et al.* v. *Des Moines Independent School District et al.*, 393 U.S. 503 (1969).
35. *Ibid.*, p. 506.
36. *Ibid.*, p. 509.
37. *Ibid.*, p. 511.
38. *Ibid.*, p. 515.
39. *Ibid.*, p. 517.
40. *Ibid.*, p. 524.
41. *Beilan, op. cit.*, p. 406.
42. Joseph E. Bryson, "Legality of Loyalty Oath and Non-Oath Requirements for Public School Teachers" (unpublished Ed.D. Dissertation, Duke University, 1961), p. 32.
43. *Cramp* v. *Board of Public Instruction of Orange County*, 368 U.S. 278 (1961).
44. *Ibid.*, p. 280.

45. *Ibid.*, p. 286.
46. *Ibid.*, p. 287.
47. Arval A. Morris, "Academic Freedom and Loyalty Oaths," *Law and Contemporary Problems*, XXXVIII (Summer, 1963), 510.
48. Charles E. Rice, *Freedom of Association* (New York: New York University Press, 1962), p. 167.
49. *Baggett v. Bullitt*, 377 U.S. 360 (1964).
50. *Ibid.*, p. 361.
51. *Ibid.*, p. 362.
52. *Ibid.*, p. 372.
53. *Ibid.*, p. 373.
54. *Ibid.*, p. 362.
55. *Elfbrandt v. Russell et al.*, 384 U.S. 11 (1966).
56. *Ibid.*, p. 12.
57. *Ibid.*, p. 13.
58. *Ibid.*, p. 16.
59. *Ibid.*, p. 17.
60. *Baggett, op. cit.*, p. 374.
61. *Whitehall v. Elkins, President, University of Maryland et al.*, 389 U.S. 54 (1967).
62. *Ibid.*, p. 55.
63. *Ibid.*, p. 59.
64. *Ibid.*, p. 61.
65. *Ibid.*, p. 63.
66. *Keyishian et al. v. Board of Regents of the University of the State of New York, et al.*, 385 U.S. 589 (1967).
67. *Ibid.*, p. 599.
68. *Ibid.*, p. 603.
69. *Ibid.*
70. *Ibid.*, p. 608.
71. *Ibid.*, p. 620.
72. *Ibid.*, p. 622.

Chapter VI

CONCLUDING SUMMARY

At the outset of this volume, the stated purpose was to examine and analyze the public school cases decided by the Supreme Court of the United States since Earl Warren became Chief Justice. Thirty-five cases have been heard by the Warren Court affecting religion, segregation, and academic freedom. A study of each of these areas brings forth this concluding summary.

Religion

The controversy over religious instruction in the public schools has led to eight suits resulting in decisions by the Warren Court. Each of the cases has involved a restricted phase of the religious question, and five concerned a mutual issue, the practice of having Bible reading and /or prayers in the school's opening exercises. The Supreme Court decided the cases on the establishment clause of the First Amendment, and the Court held that each practice was unconstitutional. The other three cases dealt with lending textbooks to children in parochial schools, teaching the Darwinian theory of evolution, and allowing individuals to contest the expenditure of federal funds. The Court upheld the textbook loan act, upheld the right to teach evolution, and paved the way for individuals to sue the government under certain conditions.

In the prayer and Bible reading decisions, the Supreme Court held that the establishment clause was violated because the state was involved in religion. No distinction was made between the state and its agency, the school, in sponsorship of the devotional activities; therefore, whether the source was the state or the school was immaterial. The real problem was that the school was supporting the activity, through use of the building, school time, or teachers. The Court's majority did not hold, however, that the religious exercises were illegal because of school financing, although the issue was raised in concurring opinions. A further involvement by the state in one of the cases was its authorship of a prayer for school use. To the justices, these instances were sufficient evidence that the state was engaged in the promotion of religion in the public schools.

A challenge to an alleged establishment of religion may be made, even when the personal injury is minor. In the cases studied, voluntary participation did not save the legality of the religious practices. Even in exercises in which there is the option of participating or not participating, there is great pressure upon young people to conform. If a child does engage in a religious exercise with which he is in disagreement, he is at a disadvantage for not being intellectually mature enough to analyze conflicting ideas and opinions, and then to form his own judgments. Whether a state statute or a local school board rule allows for voluntary participation, that fact does not constitutionally save the practice. An element of coercion, whether direct or indirect, exists which allows a complainant sufficient standing to sue.

Legislation by the majority is not in effect in matters affecting religious practices in the public schools. To hold otherwise would be to incorporate the majority's wishes into mandated exercises, and the end result would be an establishment of religion. Since equal protection is guaranteed to all persons under the Constitution, the rights of the minority must be accorded equal treatment.

A state is neutral in religion; so is the school, for the school is, in fact, the state. Belief and unbelief have equal value in a school. The state can neither advocate any religious doctrine nor use its influence in promoting an activity in the public school. Although in one of the Bible reading and prayer cases, the state had become involved through authorship of a prayer, the crucial issue was actually one of sponsorship which the establishment clause prohibits.

The Supreme Court's task of ruling on the legality of the exercises was made easier after the justices held that the Bible is sectarian. It favors some persons, it arouses hostility in some, and it is neutral to other groups. The fact that it is an instrument of some religious sects generates both advocacy for and disagreement with its doctrines. Thus, because the Bible is in conflict with some people's beliefs, use of it in the morning devotional exercises violates the establishment clause.

The opinions raised questions about the study of religion. The justices indicated that there is a place in the school curriculum for a study about religion as distinguished from a study of religion. This leaves open the question of what religion is and the extent to which study about it can be upheld under the First Amendment.

From the study and analysis of the cases and the summary treatment given, certain conclusions are drawn. In the first place, misunderstanding of or antagonism to the opinions of the Warren Court stems not so much from revolutionary decisions of substance but from the number of people affected by them. In particular, the prayer and Bible reading decisions are consistent with previous Supreme Court holdings antedating the 1953 and subsequent Court memberships. On the other hand, *Flast* opens up the possibility of a new era of litigation. The evolution decision will have very little impact on the schools as the law itself and its enforcement have not been taken seriously by school officials.

In holding that the recitation of Bible verses and prayers in the public schools is unconstitutional, the Supreme Court has not formulated nor begun a new pattern of thinking. The decisions follow the ruling of the Court in previous cases, most notably *Zorach*.

Large numbers of people gain no preferential treatment when the Supreme Court adjudicates issues involving religious practices in the public schools. All persons have equal rights under the Constitution, and a small minority will be given as much protection as a vast majority. The Court will stand as a safeguard to insure that the minority will be shielded from pressures to conform to or participate in practices with which they are in disagreement.

Not only are the decisions a victory for the minority, but they also protect other religious sects as well as nonbelievers. By virtue of this, no one group can exert its influence on a school activity, but all can pursue their mode of worship outside school.

Segregation

Public school segregation cases have involved litigation over the separation of whites and Negroes, and the Supreme Court during Earl Warren's tenure as Chief Justice has rendered thirteen decisions concerning this issue. The landmark case was the overturning of state constitutional and statutory provisions either authorizing or permitting separate schools for the two races. Following that decision the Court granted relief and heard ensuing cases concerning integration.

While declaring segregation in the public schools to be a violation of the equal protection clause of the Fourteenth Amendment, the Supreme Court recognized that education is primarily a state and local responsibility. The Court gave local school administrators broad guidelines in preparing desegregation plans consistent and in harmony with local administrative and geographic problems. The Court recognized that complete desegregation could not be realized immediately; therefore, the best equitable solution lay with local initiative and responsibility.

A time chart for desegregation set by the Supreme Court was flexible, its main guideline being "with all deliberate speed." This allowed administrative flexibility for local schools in meeting the Court's decree and in gaining public acceptance of the decision. Whereas the cases decided soon after 1954 indicated patience with local officials in effectuating desegregation policies and plans, more recent ones have shown a reluctance to accept delays.

Equal protection, as interpreted by the Supreme Court in the school segregation cases, actually means equal treatment. Persons can be classified or treated differently when consistent with or relevant to the purposes of legislation or the action involved. However, racial classifications for the purpose of school assignment do not fall within this category, as they are not pursuant to a legitimate governmental purpose. The real test is whether or not injustice results from the classifications.

Education is of more importance today to the individual and to the country than it was sixty or one hundred years ago. It is almost a prerequisite for success, for professional work, and for appreciation of cultural values. There is merit in children interacting with others educationally, for this aids in later training and in adjustment to an adult environment. A new look at education and its importance means that all children must be given an equal opportunity in school without discrimination.

As an agency of the state, the school cannot discriminate. Further, a school need not be an entirely public one to be subject to the prohibition. Where a governing board of a school is classified as an agency of the state, the school, although otherwise considered to be private, comes under the ban of the Fourteenth Amendment if it practices segregation. Discrimination is thus forbidden if its source is the state.

The Court will not tolerate administrative schemes which attempt to delay or circumvent the desegregation edict. Justices have overturned stalling tactics, transfer plans, and creation of private schools which have been designed to perpetuate segregation. The Court will not accept as constitutionally valid a state's abandoning its school system to avoid integration.

The Supreme Court has not actually ruled that there must be integration of the school children, although it has held that there cannot be discriminatory segregation. Showing that there is no discrimination in assignment of Negroes to schools rests with the local school officials.

The cases in segregation have followed a continuum rather than pronounced a completely new doctrine. Whereas previous cases before the Supreme Court dealt with individuals, the class action decisions

CONCLUDING SUMMARY   159

beginning in 1954 affected many people. However, the substance of the Court decisions has not changed. Any new doctrine found in the segregation decisions is the concept of the state's role in education. Where a degree of state action is involved in the management of a school, that school is subject to the desegregation pronouncements. The Court will go far in aiding the Negro to strike down barriers preventing his attending a desegregated school. Again, this gives protection to a minority group.

Academic Freedom

The third area of study, academic freedom, dealt with the freedom of a teacher to hold membership in organizations and to refuse to take loyalty oaths. The Supreme Court heard seven cases touching on freedom of speech and association, and five dealing with loyalty oaths. The five oath laws were declared to be unconstitutional, while the litigation concerning teacher affiliation with organizations was decided on the narrow issues of the individual case. Free speech protection was granted to both teacher and pupil in two separate cases. Two factors hamper the drawing of broad constitutional principles from the context within which the cases were decided. Many of the decisions involved a 5-4 voting of the Court, indicating a lack of agreement among the justices about the issues. Further, cases before the Supreme Court in this area are of such recent origin that there are not many precedents upon which to draw.

On the basis of the five loyalty oath cases, the Supreme Court has held that, if an oath law is to be sustained, it must be susceptible to objective measurement. Its meaning must be sufficiently clear so that persons bound by it will know when the law is being violated. When one has to guess at the intent of the statute, it is too vague and broad to be upheld. The mere fact that one is required to swear to abstain from advocating the overthrow of the government by force or violence does not mean he is committing a crime.

Associational freedom is protected in part by the due process clause of the Fourteenth Amendment, but to a greater degree by the right of assembly of the First Amendment. Problems turning on this freedom relate to a teacher's membership in proscribed organizations and the degree to which a teacher can be interrogated about these activities. From the cases and within the narrow context of the decisions rendered, principles have been extracted which give some guides.

Many factors determine a teacher's fitness, and persons who employ teachers may make investigations to determine their competency to instruct young people. A teacher should be candid in answering questions of his employer, or insubordination may result.

Questioning of teachers, however, can be too indiscriminate. It should be made clear as to what the investigation entails; further, the inquiry should serve a legitimate interest of the state. An investigation which subjects one to questions about a broad range of activities can provoke two evils. It may be unrelated to one's competency to teach and it can possibly result in information's being used against the person. Therefore, a teacher need not answer all questions about previous associational memberships and ties if they are unrelated to his suitability as a teacher.

The Un-American Activities Committee of the United States House of Representatives may conduct investigations about teachers, as the Warren Court extended the scope of the committee's investigation to public education. Here, the inquiry into this field was deemed to serve the public interest more than it was to protect the freedom of the individual.

Dismissal of teachers for violation of statutes restricting their activities must follow prescribed rules. This includes a hearing wherein a teacher is given an opportunity to defend his actions.

A teacher may hold innocent membership in an organization listed as being subversive. The Court will protect him from being dismissed for the unknowing character of the organization at the time he joined.

In academic freedom the conclusion is that the Supreme Court has not settled the balance-of-interest concept—that is, which is the more important, the interest of the state or the freedom of the individual teacher. The Court has indicated a desire to guarantee both, which has resulted in deciding each case as it arises.

TABLE OF CASES

1. *Adler et al. v. Board of Education of the City of New York*, 342 U.S. 485 (1952) 42, 120
2. *Baggett v. Bullitt*, 377 U.S. 360 (1964) 142
3. *Barenblatt v. United States*, 360 U.S. 109 (1959) 127
4. *Beilan v. Board of Public Education, School District of Philadelphia*, 357 U.S. 399 (1958) 125
5. *Board of Education of Central School District No. 1. et al. v. Allen, Commissioner of Education of New York, et al.*, 392 U.S. 236 (1968) 37
6. *Bolling et al. v. Sharpe et al.*, 347 U.S. 497 (1954) 80
7. *Briggs v. Elliott*, 103 F. Supp. 920 (1952) 77
8. *Brown et al. v. Board of Education of Topeka, et al.*, 349 U.S. 294 (1955) 81
9. *Brown et al. v. Board of Education of Topeka et al.*, 347 U.S. 483 (1954) 76
10. *Cantwell v. Connecticut*, 310 U.S. 296 (1940) 25
11. *Chamberlin et al. v. Dade County Board of Public Instruction et al.*, 377 U.S. 402 (1964) 35
12. *Cochran v. Louisiana State Board of Education*, 281 U.S. 370 (1930) 8
13. *Cooper et al., Members of the Board of Directors of the Little Rock, Arkansas, Independent School District, et al. v. Aaron et al.*, 358 U.S. 1 (1958) 83
14. *Cramp v. Board of Public Instruction of Orange County*, 368 U.S. 278 (1961) 140
15. *Cumming v. Board of Education of Richmond County*, 175 U.S. 528 (1899) 16, 79
16. *Davis v. County School Board of Prince Edward County*, 103 F. Supp. 337 (1952) 77
17. *Doremus et al. v. Board of Education of the Borough of Hawthorne et al.*, 342 U.S. 429 (1952) 13
18. *Elfbrandt v. Russell et al.*, 384 U.S. 11 (1966) 143
19. *Engel v. Vitale*, 370 U.S. 421 (1962) 27
20. *Epperson et al. v. State of Arkansas*, 393 U.S. 97 (1968) 41

21. *Everson v. Board of Education of Ewing Township*, 330 U.S. 1 (1947)... 9
22. *Ferrell et al. v. Dallas Independent School District et al.*, 393 U.S. 856 (1968) 133
23. *Flast et al. v. Cohen, Secretary of Health, Education, and Welfare, et al.*, 392 U.S. 83 (1968) 40
24. *Frothingham v. Mellon*, 262 U.S. 447 (1923) 40
25. *Garner v. Board of Public Works of Los Angeles et al.*, 341 U.S. 716 (1951) 20
26. *Gebhart v. Belton*, 91 A. (2d) 137 (1952) 77
27. *Georgia v. Tennessee Copper Company*, 206 U.S. 230 (1907) .. 97
28. *Gong Lum et al. v. Rice et al.*, 275 U.S. 78 (1927)................ 17, 79
29. *Goss et al. v. Board of Education of Knoxville, Tennessee, et al.*, 373 U.S. 683 (1963) 85
30. *Green et al. v. County School Board of New Kent County et al.*, 391 U.S. 430 (1968) 90
31. *Griffin et al. v. County School Board of Prince Edward County et al.*, 377 U.S. 218 (1964).. 88
32. *Illinois ex rel. McCollum v. Board of Education of School District No. 71, Champaign County, Illinois et al.*, 333 U.S. 203 (1948).. 12
33. *Jones v. Opelika*, 316 U.S. 584 (1942) 11
34. *Keyishian et al. v. Board of Regents of the University of the State of New York et al.*, 385 U.S. 589 (1967)........................ 145
35. *Lochner v. New York*, 198 U.S. 45 (1905)............................... 102
36. *McLaurin v. Oklahoma State Regents for Higher Education et al.*, 339 U.S. 637 (1950) 18, 75
37. *McNeese et al. v. Board of Education for Community Unit School District 187, Cahokia, Illinois, et al.*, 373 U.S. 668 (1963) 85
38. *Minersville School District, Board of Education of Minersville School District et al. v. Gobitis et al.*, 310 U.S. 586 (1940) 10
39. *Missouri ex rel. Gaines v. Canada, Registrar of the University of Missouri, et al.*, 305 U.S. 337 (1938) 18, 74
40. *Monroe et al. v. Board of Commissioners of the City of Jackson et al.*, 391 U.S. 450 (1968)... 90
41. *Muller v. Oregon*, 208 U.S. 412 (1908)..................................... 102
42. *Murray et al. v. Curlett et al., Constituting the Board of Commissioners of Baltimore City*, 179 A. (2d) 698 (1962) 30
43. *Pennsylvania et al. v. Board of Directors of City Trusts of the City of Philadelphia*, 353 U.S. 230 (1957) 82

TABLE OF CASES

44. *Pickering* v. *Board of Education of Township High School District 205, Will County, Illinois*, 391 U.S. 563 (1968)............ 132
45. *Pierce* v. *Society of Sisters (and Hill Military Academy)*, 268 U.S. 510 (1925) 9
46. *Plessy* v. *Ferguson*, 163 U.S. 537 (1896)................................. 14, 74
47. *Quick Bear* v. *Leupp*, 210 U.S. 50 (1908) 7
48. *Raney et al.* v. *Board of Education of the Gould School District et al.*, 391 U.S. 443 (1968) 90
49. *Rogers et al.* v. *Paul et al.*, 382 U.S. 198 (1965) 90
50. *School District of Abington Township, Pennsylvania, et al.* v. *Schempp et al.*, 374 U.S. 203 (1963) 29
51. *Shelton et al.* v. *Tucker et al.*, 364 U.S. 479 (1960)................. 129
52. *Sipuel* v. *Board of Regents of the University of Oklahoma et al.*, 332 U.S. 631 (1948) 18, 74
53. *Slochower* v. *Board of Higher Education of New York City*, 350 U.S. 551 (1956)... 122
54. *Standard Oil Company* v. *United States*, 221 U.S. 1 (1910).... 97
55. *Stein* v. *Oshinsky, Principal, Public School 184, Whitestone, New York, et al.*, 382 U.S. 957 (1965) 37
56. *Sweatt* v. *Painter et al.*, 339 U.S. 629 (1950)......................... 18, 75
57. *Sweezy* v. *New Hampshire, by Wyman, Attorney General*, 354 U.S. 234 (1957)... 123
58. *Tinker et al.* v. *Des Moines Independent School District et al.*, 393 U.S. 503 (1969) 134
59. *United States* v. *American Tobacco Company*, 221 U.S. 106 (1911)... 98
60. *United States* v. *Montgomery County Board of Education*, 395 U.S. 225 (1969)... 93
61. *West Virginia State Board of Education et al.* v. *Barnette et al.*, 319 U.S. 624 (1943) 11
62. *Whitehall* v. *Elkins, President, University of Maryland et al.*, 389 U.S. 54 (1967) 144
63. *Wieman et al.* v. *Updegraff et al.*, 344 U.S. 183 (1952)........... 21
64. *Zorach et al.* v. *Clauson et al., Constituting the Board of Education of the City of New York et al.*, 343 U.S. 306 (1952). 13

SELECTED BIBLIOGRAPHY

Books

Berman, Harold J. (ed.). *Talks on American Law.* New York: Vintage Books, 1961.

Berns, Walter. *Virtue and the First Amendment.* Baton Rouge: Louisiana State University Press, 1957.

Blanshard, Paul. *Religion and the Schools: The Great Controversy.* Boston: Beacon Press, 1963.

Blaustein, Albert P., and Clarence Clyde Ferguson, Jr. *Desegregation and the Law.* New Brunswick, N.J.: Rutgers University Press, 1957.

Boles, Donald E. *The Bible, Religion, and the Public Schools.* (3rd ed.) Ames, Iowa: Iowa State University Press, 1965.

──────. *The Two Swords: Commentaries and Cases in Religion and Education.* Ames, Iowa: Iowa State University Press, 1967.

Bolmeier, Edward C. *The School in the Legal Structure.* Cincinnati: The W. H. Anderson Company, 1968.

Burns, James MacGregor, and Jack Walter Peltason. *Government by the People.* (3rd ed.) Englewood Cliffs, N.J.: Prentice-Hall, Inc., 1957.

Cushman, Robert E. *Civil Liberties in the United States: A Guide to Current Problems and Experiences.* Ithaca, N.Y.: Cornell University Press, 1956.

Dierenfield, Richard B. *Religion in American Public Schools.* Washington, D.C.: Public Affairs Press, 1962.

Duker, Sam. *Schools and Religion: The Legal Context.* New York: Harper and Row, Publishers, 1966.

Edwards, Newton, *The Courts and the Public Schools: The Legal Basis of School Organization and Administration.* (Rev. ed.) Chicago: The University of Chicago Press, 1955.

Fairchild, Henry Pratt. *The Anatomy of Freedom.* New York: Philosophical Library, Inc., 1957.

Fellman, David, *The Constitutional Right of Association.* Chicago: The University of Chicago Press, 1963.

──────. *The Limits of Freedom.* New Brunswick, N.J.: Rutgers University Press, 1959.

────────── (ed.). *The Supreme Court and Education.* New York: Bureau of Publications, Teachers College, Columbia University, 1960.
Greenberg, Jack. *Race Relations and American Law.* New York: Columbia University Press, 1959.
Griffiths, William E. *Religion, the Courts and the Public Schools.* Cincinnati: The W. H. Anderson Company, 1966.
Harris, Robert J. *The Quest for Equality: The Constitution, Congress and the Supreme Court.* Baton Rouge: Louisiana State University Press, 1960.
Kauper, Paul G. *Civil Liberties and the Constitution.* Ann Arbor: The University of Michigan Press, 1962.
Peterson, Leroy, Jr., Richard A. Rossmiller, and Marlin M. Volz. *The Law and Public School Operation.* New York: Harper and Row, Publishers, 1969.
Religion in the Public Schools. Washington, D.C.: American Association of School Administrators, 1964.
Rice, Charles E. *Freedom of Association.* New York: New York University Press, 1962.
────────── . *The Supreme Court and Public Prayer: The Need for Restraint.* New York: Fordham University Press, 1964.
Sizer, Theodore R. (ed.). *Religion and Public Education.* New York: Houghton Mifflin Company, 1967.
Spurlock, Clark. *Education and the Supreme Court.* Urbana: University of Illinois Press, 1955.
Thayer, V. T. *The Attack Upon the American Secular School.* Boston: The Beacon Press, 1951.

Unpublished Dissertation

Bryson, Joseph E. "Legality of Loyalty Oath and Non-Oath Requirements for Public School Teachers." Unpublished Ed.D. Dissertation, Duke University, 1961.

Legal Periodicals

Angel, Charles F. "Integration in Public Schools," *Montana Law Review,* XX (Fall, 1958), 126-131.
Borinski, Ernst. "A Legal and Social Analysis of the Integration Decrees of May 31, 1955," *University of Pittsburgh Law Review,* XVI (Summer, 1955), 329-338.
────────── . "A Legal and Sociological Analysis of the Segregation Decision of May 17, 1954," *University of Pittsburgh Law Review,* XV (Summer, 1954), 622-634.

SELECTED BIBLIOGRAPHY

Calhoun, Philo. "School Prayer in Short Perspective," *Connecticut Bar Journal*, XXVIII (December, 1964), 643-654.

Canavan, Francis. "Implications of the School Prayer and Bible Reading Decisions: The Welfare State," *Journal of Public Law*, XIII (1964), 439-446.

Choper, Jesse H. "Religion in the Public Schools: A Proposed Constitutional Standard," *Minnesota Law Review*, XLVII (January, 1963), 329-416.

Clark, Elias. "Charitable Trusts, the Fourteenth Amendment and the Will of Stephen Girard," *The Yale Law Journal*, LXVI (June, 1957), 979-1015.

Cushman, Robert Fairchild. "The Holy Bible and the Public Schools," *Cornell Law Review*, XL (Spring, 1955), 475-499.

Davis, Wylie H. "The School Segregation Decisions: A Legal Analysis," *Journal of Public Law*, III (Spring, 1954), 83-89.

DeLacy, George L. "The Segregation Cases: A Judicial Problem Judicially Solved," *American Bar Association Journal*, XLIII (June, 1957), 519-521.

Dixon, Robert G. "Religion, Schools, and the Open Society: A Socio-Constitutional Issue," *Journal of Public Law*, XIII (1964), 267-309.

Dunsford, John E. "The Establishment Syndrome and Religious Liberty," *Duquesne University Law Review*, II (Summer, 1964), 139-212.

Fellman, David. "Religion in American Education," *Boston University Law Review*, XLIV (1964), 287-299.

Frantz, Laurent B. "The School Segregation Cases," *Lawyer's Guild Review*, XIV (Summer, 1954), 59-64.

Fuchs, Ralph F. "Academic Freedom—Its Basic Philosophy, Function, and History," *Law and Contemporary Problems*, XXVIII (Summer, 1963), 431-446.

Hanft, Frank W. "The Prayer Decision," *North Carolina Law Review*, XLII (1964), 567-599.

Harrison, Joseph W. "The Bible, the Constitution, and Public Education," *Tennessee Law Review*, XXIX (Spring, 1962), 363-418.

Hartmen, Paul. "The United States Supreme Court and Desegregation," *The Modern Law Review*, XXIII (July, 1960), 353-372.

Heyman, Ira Michael. "The Chief Justice, Racial Segregation, and the Friendly Critics," *California Law Review*, XLIX (March, 1961), 104-125.

Howe, Mark De Wolfe. "Religion and Race in Public Education," *Buffalo Law Review*, VIII (Winter, 1959), 242-250.

"Implementation of the Segregation Decision," *Northwestern University Law Review*, XLIX (September-October, 1954), 557-566.

"Judicial Disestablishment in Public Education," *Northwestern University Law Review,* LVII (November-December, 1962), 578-595.

Kauper, Paul G. "Segregation in Public Education: The Decline of *Plessy* v. *Ferguson,*" *Michigan Law Review,* LII (June, 1954), 1137-1158.

Knowles, Laurence W. "School Desegregation," *North Carolina Law Review,* XLII (December, 1963), 67-85.

Ladd, Edward T. "Public Education and Religion," *Journal of Public Law,* XIII (1964), 310-342.

Lewis, Robert E. "Transfer of Public Trust to Private Trustees Permits Continued School Segregation," *Ohio State Law Journal,* XX (Winter, 1959), 132-136.

Maher, Richard M. "The Supreme Court and Segregation," *University of Detroit Law Journal,* XVIII (November, 1954), 64-73.

McKay, Robert B. " 'With All Deliberate Speed' A Study of School Desegregation," *New York University Law Review,* XXXI (July, 1956), 991-1090.

McWhinney, Edward. "An End to Racial Discrimination in the United States?," *Canadian Bar Review,* XXXII (May, 1954), 545-566.

Milbourn, Don L. "De Facto Segregation and the Neighborhood School," *Wayne Law Review,* IX (Spring, 1963), 514-523.

Moore, John Norton. "The Supreme Court and the Relationship Between the 'Establishment' and 'Free Exercise' Clauses," *Texas Law Review,* XLII (1964), 142-198.

Morris, Arval A. "Academic Freedom and Loyalty Oaths," *Law and Contemporary Problems,* XXVIII (Summer, 1963), 487-514.

Murphy, William P. "Academic Freedom—An Emerging Constitutional Right," *Law and Contemporary Problems,* XXVIII (Summer, 1963), 447-486.

Palmer, Charles L. "The Fourteenth Amendment: Some Reflections on Segregation in Schools," *American Bar Association Journal,* XLIX (July, 1963), 645-651.

Pollak, Louis H. "Public Prayers in Public Schools." *Harvard Law Review,* LXXVII (November, 1963), 62-78.

Regan, Richard J. "The Dilemma of Religious Instruction and the Public Schools," *The Catholic Lawyer,* X (Winter, 1964), 42-54, 82.

Ribaudo, Anthony P. "Segregation in Education," *Boston University Law Review,* XXXIV (November, 1954), 463-478.

Rogers, William P. "The Problem of School Segregation: A Serious Challenge to American Citizens," *American Bar Association Journal,* XLV (January, 1959), 23-26.

Rosenfield, Harry N. "Separation of Church and State in the Public

Schools," *University of Pittsburgh Law Review,* XXII (March, 1961), 561-589.

Sanders, Paul H. "The School Segregation Cases: A Comment," *Vanderbilt Law Review,* VII (August, 1954), 985-996.

Schwartz, Larry H. "Separation of Church and State: Religious Exercises in the Schools," *University of Cincinnati Law Review,* XXXI (Fall, 1962), 408-434.

Sedler, Robert Allen. "School Segregation in the North and West: Legal Aspects," *Saint Louis University Law Journal,* VII (Spring, 1963), 228-275.

"The 'Separate But Equal' Doctrine and the Segregation Cases," *Albany Law Review,* XIX (June, 1955), 233-250.

Shanks, Hershel. " 'State Action' and the Girard Estate Case," *University of Pennsylvania Law Review,* CV (December, 1956), 213-240.

"The Supreme Court, the First Amendment, and Religion in the Public Schools," *Columbia Law Review,* LXIII (January, 1963), 73-97.

Waite, Edward F. "Race Segregation in the Public Schools: Jim Crow at the Judgment Seat," *Minnesota Law Review,* XXXVIII (May, 1954), 612-621.

Weclaw, Robert G. "The Establishment Clause and 'Coercion,' " *Marquette Law Review,* XLVII (1963-1964), 359-367.

Educational Periodicals

Abraham, Henry J. "Freedom of Expression: A Constant Dilemma," *Social Education,* XXIII (December, 1959), 364-370, 382.

Bolmeier, E. C. "Legality and Propriety of Religious Instruction in the Public Schools," *The Educational Forum,* XX (May, 1956), 473-482.

Byse, Clark. "Teachers and the Fifth Amendment," *American Association of University Professors Bulletin,* XLI (Autumn, 1955), 456-475.

Caliver, Ambrose. "Education of Negroes: Segregation Issue Before the Supreme Court," *School Life,* XXXVI (February, 1954), 74-76, 78.

Clift, Virgil A. "The History of Racial Segregation in American Education," *School and Society,* LXXXVIII (May 7, 1960), 220-229.

Collier, James M., and John J. George. "Education and the Supreme Court," *The Journal of Higher Education,* XXI (January, 1950), 77-83.

Doak, Dale. "Do Court Decisions Give Minority Rule?," *Phi Delta Kappan,* XLV (October, 1963), 20-24.

Duker, Sam. "The Supreme Court Ruling on School Prayers," *The Educational Forum,* XXVII (November, 1962), 71-77.

Fuchs, Ralph F. "The Barenblatt Decision and the Supreme Court and the Academic Profession," *American Association of University Professors Bulletin,* XLV (September, 1959), 333-338.

———. "Intellectual Freedom and the Educational Process," *American Association of University Professors Bulletin,* XLII (Autumn, 1956), 471-481.

Garber, Lee O. "Court Bars Bible Reading, But Finds Place for Religion in Schools," *The Nation's Schools,* LXXII (August, 1963), 50-51.

———. "Four Big Educational Issues Dominate Court Cases," *The Nation's Schools,* LXXIII (March, 1964), 76-77, 126-130.

———. "Four Church-State Controversies: How They Affect Education," *The Nation's Schools,* LXIX (June, 1962), 66-68.

———. "Prayer Barred: What It Means," *The Nation's Schools,* LXX (August, 1962), 54-55, 76.

———. "U.S. Supreme Court Takes Middle of the Road on Segregation," *The Nation's Schools,* LVI (July, 1955), 71-72.

———. "What the Courts Say About Segregation," *The Nation's Schools,* XLIX (May, 1952), 78-81.

Hoffman, Robert, "A Note on Academic Freedom," *Phi Delta Kappan,* XLIV (January, 1963), 185-188.

Hudgins, H. C., Jr. "Desegregation: Where Schools Stand with the Courts As the New Year Begins," *The American School Board Journal,* CLVI (January, 1969), 21-25.

———, and Robert A. Nelson. "Prayer, the Bible, and the Public Schools," *North Carolina Education,* XXXIII (October, 1966), 12-13, 43-45.

Hunt, R. L. "How Schools Can Teach Religious Values—Legally," *The Nation's Schools,* LXXIII (February, 1964), 48-49.

Mark, Max. "The Meanings of Academic Freedom," *American Association of University Professors Bulletin,* XLIII (September, 1957), 498-506.

Morrow, Glenn R. "Academic Freedom," *American Association of University Professors Bulletin,* XL (Winter, 1954-1955), 529-535.

Murphy, William P. "Educational Freedom in the Courts," *American Association of University Professors Bulletin,* XL (December, 1963), 309-327.

Paul, James C. N. "The Litigious Future of Desegregation," *Educational Leadership,* XIII (October, 1955), 110-116.

Picott, J. Rupert, and Edward H. Peeples, Jr. "Prince Edward County, Virginia," *Phi Delta Kappan,* XLV (May, 1964), 393-397.

Punke, Harold H. "Constitutional and Legal Aspects of the Church-State-School Problem," *School and Society,* LXXXIX (May 6, 1961), 222-226.

Puryear, Paul L. "Equity Power and the School Desegregation Cases," *Harvard Educational Review*, XXXIII (Fall, 1963), 421-438.
Sanders, Thomas G. "Religious Freedom: The Court Expands a Concept," *The Nation*, CXCVII (July 13, 1963), 25-28.
Starr, Isidore. "Recent Supreme Court Decisions: Academic Freedom," *Social Education*, XXI (December, 1957), 349-352, 354.
—————. "Recent Supreme Court Decisions: Freedom of Association of Teachers," *Social Education*, XXV (November, 1961), 357-360.
—————. "Recent Supreme Court Decisions: Separation of Church and State," *Social Education*, XXVII (December, 1962), 439-444.
Steinhilber, August W. "Florida Loyalty Oath Unconstitutional," *School Life*, XLIV (January-February, 1962), 22.
—————. "Loyalty Oaths Before the Court," *School Life*, XLIV (October, 1961), 14-17.
—————. "Supreme Court Decision on Government-Sponsored Prayer," *School Life*, XLIV (July, 1962), 8-9.
Stevenson, William E. "Education and Freedom," *School and Society*, LXXXIV (December 22, 1956), 211-213.
Sutherland, Arthur E. "The Supreme Court and Private Schools," *Harvard Educational Review*, XXV (Summer, 1955), 127-131.
Thayer, V. T. "Public Aid to Religious Education," *School and Society*, LXXXIX (May 6, 1961), 226-230.
Valenti, Jasper J., Paul A. Woelfl and James O'Shaughnessy. "A Double Revolution: The Supreme Court's Desegregation Decision," *Harvard Educational Review*, XXV (Winter, 1955), 1-17.

Pamphlets and Newspaper Articles

Douglas, William O. *Freedom of the Mind*. New York: American Library Association, 1962.
"High Court Bans School Segregation: 9-to-0 Decision Grants Time to Comply," *New York Times*, CIII, No. 35,178 (May 18, 1954), 1, 14.
Johnson, F. Ernest. "A Problem of Culture," *Religion and the Schools*. New York: The Fund for the Republic, 1959.
"Legislative Committee May Not Inquire Into Subject Matter of Teacher's Lectures," *The National School Law Reporter*, R. R. Hamilton (ed.). New London, Connecticut: Arthur C. Croft Publications, VIII, No. 24 (February 12, 1959), 93-96.
"The Regents Statement on Moral and Spiritual Training in the Schools," *The University of the State of New York Bulletin to the Schools*, XXXVIII (December, 1951), 94.

INDEX OF TOPICS

Academic freedom
 (See subject headings in Chapter V)
Adler, Irving, 21
Alabama, state of, 93
America (song), 65
American Tobacco Company, 98
Amici Curiae, 80, 93
Arizona, state of, 143
Arkansas, state of, 41, 42, 90, 92, 129
Armbands, 134
Assembly programs, 64
Assignment to school
 Cahokia, Illinois, 86
 Gould, Arkansas, 92
 Jackson, Tennessee, 92
 Knoxville, Tennessee, 85
 Mississippi, 17
 New Kent County, Virginia, 91

Baccalaureate programs, 35-37, 63
Baltimore, city of, 30
Baltimore School Board, 30
Beilan, Herman, 125
Bible
 Reading of, 13, 29, 30, 34, 35
 Teaching from, 67
 Version used, 30, 59
Bill of attainder, 20, 21
Black, Justice
 Adler decision, 22
 Allen decision, 38, 39
 Barenblatt decision, 128
 Beilan decision, 127
 Elfbrandt decision, 143
 Engel decision, 27-29, 45, 46, 50, 52-54, 56, 57, 62
 Epperson decision, 41, 42
 Everson decision, 9, 44
 Griffin decision, 88, 89, 99, 105, 108, 110
 Incorporation of Establishment Clause into the Fourteenth Amendment, 25
 Keyishian decision, 146
 Length of service, 1

McCollum decision, 12
Montgomery decision, 94
Sweezy decision, 124
Tinker decision, 136
Blaustein, Albert P., 106
Board of Regents, 21, 145
Book of Common Prayer, 28, 29, 45
Brandeis, Justice, 102
Brennan, Justice
 Barenblatt decision, 128
 Beilan decision, 127
 Brown ('54) decision, 109
 Elfbrandt decision, 143
 Green decision, 90, 91
 Keyishian decision, 146, 147
 Schempp decision, 31, 33, 49, 50, 62
 Sweezy decision, 124
Brown, Justice, 15, 74
Brown, Linda, 76
Buffalo, University of, 145
Bureau of Catholic Indian Missions, 7, 8
Burton, Justice, 9, 123-126
Byrnes, Justice, 11

Cahokia, Illinois, 86
Canavan, Francis, 56
Central High School, Little Rock, Arkansas, 41, 83
Census
 Federal, 105
 Religious, 35-37
Centreville School, Illinois, 86
Certiorari, 2, 37, 53, 86, 133
Champaign, Illinois, 12
Chapel exercises, 64
Chase, Justice, 1
Chief Justice
 Assignment, writing opinions, 4
 Initiator of arguments, 3
 Number of chief justices, 4
 Seating according to seniority, 3
Child benefit theory
 Principle of, 14
 Textbooks, 8, 38
 Transportation, 9

173

Christmas
  Celebrations, 35, 36
  Plays, 35
Church membership, 55
Clark, Justice
  Elfbrandt decision, 143
  Garner decision, 20
  Goss decision, 85, 86, 98
  Griffin decision, 90
  Keyishian decision, 146-148
  Schempp decision, 31, 32, 48, 52, 54, 55, 57, 58, 62
  Shelton decision, 131
  Slochower decision, 122, 123
  Sweezy decision, 124, 125
  Wieman decision, 21
Class action, 95
Clerk of Court, 2
Clerks, law, 2
Committee on Un-American Activities, 126, 127
Communism
  Religion as an antidote for, 36
  Legislation curbing, 128
Communist Party prohibitions
  Arizona statute, 143
  Los Angeles ordinance, 20
  New Hampshire statute, 124
  New York City charter, 122
  New York state statute, 144
  Oath laws in general, 139, 140
  Oklahoma statute, 21
  Orange County, Florida, law, 140
  Philadelphia inquiry, 126
  Washington state statute, 142
Constitution of United States
  Amendment I, 25
  Amendment XIV, 73
  Article III, 1
  Color blind, 16
  Framers of, 33
Constitutional protection, 139
Cooperation with investigating officials, 138
Council on Religious Education, 12
Course content, 124

Darwin's theory, 41
Declaration of Independence, 65
Delaware, 76, 77, 97
Deliberate speed, 82, 89
De Minimis, 51
Dierenfield, Richard B., 63
Dismissal action, 138
District of Columbia, 80, 97
Douglas, Justice
  Adler decision, 22, 120

Allen decision, 38, 39
Beilan decision, 127, 128
Elfbrandt decision, 143
Engel decision, 27, 29, 47, 59, 60
Ferrell appeal, 133
Flast decision, 40
Keyishian decision, 146
Length of service, 1
McNeese decision, 87
Schempp decision, 31, 33, 48, 49, 60, 61
Sweezy decision, 124
Whitehall decision, 144
Zorach decision, 13
Due process, 10, 12, 80

Easter, 35, 36
Eckhardt, Christopher, 134
Elementary and Secondary Education Act, 40
Epperson, Susan, 41
Equity, 95
Error, writ of, 2
Establishment clause
  Explanation of, 43
  Justice Black's dictum, 44
  Violation of, 12
  (See also individual cases in Chapter III)
Evolution, 41
Ewing Township, New Jersey, 9
Excusal of students from prayer exercises, 27, 30, 53
Ex post facto law, 20, 21
Extent of investigation, 139

Faculty desegregation, 93
Feinberg certificate, 146, 147
Feinberg law, 21, 145
Ferguson, Clarence Clyde, Jr., 106
Field, Justice, 1
Field School, Arkansas, 92
Fifth Amendment, invoking of, 122, 123
First Amendment
  Alleged violation of, 27
  Incorporated into Fourteenth Amendment, 25
  Interpretation of, 9
Flag salute, 10, 11
Florida, state of, 35, 37, 140
Fort Smith, Arkansas, 90
Fortas, Justice
  Allen decision, 38, 39
  Elfbrandt decision, 143
  Epperson decision, 41, 42, 57
  Flast decision, 40

INDEX OF TOPICS

Keyishian decision, 146
Resignation from Supreme Court, 4
Rogers decision, 90
Tinker decision, 134, 135
Fourteenth Amendment
  Quoted, 73
  Relationship to education, 79
  Violation of, 8, 10
Frankfurter, Justice
  Adler decision, 22
  Barnette decision, 11
  Beilan decision, 127
  Cooper decision, 85
  Engel decision, 27
  Everson decision, 9
  Gobitis decision, 10
  Shelton decision, 131
  Sweezy decision, 124, 125
Free exercise, explanation of, 43
Freedom of choice plans, 90, 91

Gaines, Lloyd, 18
Garber, Lee O., 96, 97
Georgia, state of, 16
Gettysburg Address, 66
Girard College, 82, 103
Girard, Stephen, 82
Gobitis, Lillian, 10
Gobitis, Walter, 10
Goldberg, Justice, 31, 33, 62
Gould School, Arkansas, 92
Government aid to religion, 59
Government restrictions on association, 121
Grayzel, Solomon, 58

Hair cuts, 133
Hamilton, R. R., 125
Hanukkah, 36
Harlan, Justice (elder)
  Cumming decision, 17
  Plessy decision, 16, 107
  Service on the Supreme Court, 1
Harlan, Justice (younger)
  Allen decision, 38
  Barenblatt decision, 127, 128
  Brown ('54) decision, 109
  Elfbrandt decision, 143
  Epperson decision, 41, 42
  Flast decision, 40
  Griffin decision, 90
  Keyishian decision, 146
  McNeese decision, 87
  Schempp decision, 31, 33
  Shelton decision, 131

Slochower decision, 123
Sweezy decision, 124
Tinker decision, 136
Whitehall decision, 145
Hoffman, Robert, 119
Holidays, religious, 66
Holmes, Justice, 1
Hughes, Justice, 8, 18
Hunt, R. L., 68

Illinois, state of, 86, 132
Implementation of desegregation decision, 81
Inequality of black schools, 16
Inferiority of races, 101
Injunction, 16
Inquiry, pertinence of, 138
Investigation of teachers
  Affiliation with organizations, 129
  Association with Communist Party, 122
  Association with Communist Political Association, 125
  By Congress, 127
  Contents of lecture, 123

Jackson, Justice, 9, 11
Jackson, Tennessee, 92
Jefferson Davis High School, Alabama, 93
Jefferson, Thomas, 28
Johnson, F. Ernest, 68
Johnson, Justice, 1
Jurisdiction
  Appellate, 2
  Original, 1

Kansas, state of, 76, 77, 97
Kauper, Paul G., 111, 131
Knoxville, Tennessee, 85
Koran, 30

Law schools
  Comparison of, 19
  Missouri, 18, 74
  Oklahoma, 18, 74, 75
  Texas, 18, 19, 75
Leupp, Francis E., 8
Little Rock, Arkansas, 41, 83, 129
Lord's Prayer, 13, 29, 30, 59
Los Angeles, 20
Louisiana, 15
Lum, Martha, 17

McCollum, Vashti, 12
McLaurin, G. W., 18
McLean, Justice, 1
McReynolds, Justice, 10
Madison, James, 28, 47
Mandamus, 12, 17
Marshal of Supreme Court, 3
Marshall, Justice John, 1
Marshall, Justice Thurgood, 132, 133
Maryland, University of, 144
Michigan, University of, 127
Milbourn, Don L., 111
Minersville School District, Pennsylvania, 10
Minton, Justice, 21, 22, 123
Mississippi, state of, 17, 18, 42
Missouri, state of, 18, 74
Montgomery County, Alabama, 93
Morris, Arval A., 141
Murphy, Justice, 11
Murphy, William P., 129
Murray, Bill, 30
Murray, Madalyn, 30
Music, religious, 63

National Anthem, 65
National Association for the Advancement of Colored People, 129
National Guard, 83, 84
New Hampshire, state of, 124
New Jersey, state of, 9, 13
New Kent County, Virginia, 91
New York, state of, 38
New York City, 13, 21, 37

Oath laws
    Arizona, 143
    Florida, 140
    Limitations of, 22
    Los Angeles, 20
    Maryland, 144
    New York, 145
    Oklahoma, 21
    Washington, 142
Ober Act, 144
Oklahoma, state of, 18, 21, 74, 75
Oklahoma State Agricultural and Mechanical College, 21
Old Testament, 13
Orange County, Florida, 140
Oregon, state of, 9

Parochial schools
    Government aid, 7, 8, 9
    Services under ESEA, 40

State attendance requirements, 9
    Value of, 38
Patriotism
    Exercises, 65
    Flag salute, 10
    Legislation of, 11
    Recitation of historical documents, 62
Paul, James C. N., 109
Pennsylvania, state of, 10, 29, 30
Per curiam opinions
    Chamberlin, 37
    Girard, 82
    Rogers, 90
    Sipuel, 18
Pickering, Marvin, 132
Pledge of Allegiance, 10, 65
Plessy, Homer, 15
Prince Edward County, Virginia, 88
Prince Edward School Foundation, 88
Private schools
    Girard College, 82
    In Prince Edward County, Virginia, 88
    In Richmond County, Georgia, 16
Public schools
    Attendance required at, 9
    Closing of, 16, 88

Reed, Justice, 48
Regents Prayer, 27, 50
Religion
    Cooperation of church and state, 13
    Displays, 67
    Financing of, 29
    Study about, 62
    Teaching of, 112
    (See also subject headings in Chapter III)
Rice, Charles E., 141
Richmond County, Georgia, 16
Roberts, Justice, 25
Rogers, Attorney General, 98
Rutledge, Justice, 9

Sanders, Paul H., 111
Screening of teachers, 137
Sects, number of religious, 56
Sedition, 146
Sedler, Robert Allen, 112
Segregation, constitutional and statutory provisions for, 76-78
    (See also subject headings in Chapter IV)
"Separate but equal" doctrine
    Acceptance of, 16

INDEX OF TOPICS

Clarification of, 17, 19, 75, 79
Origin, 15
Separation of church and state, explanation of, 26, 44
Shanks, Hershel, 104
Sioux Indians, 7
Sipuel, Ada Lois, 18
Sousa Junior High School, District of Columbia, 80
South Carolina, state of, 76, 77
Speech, freedom of
   Students, 134
   Teachers, 132
Standard Oil Company, 97
Standing to sue, 37, 40, 41, 51
"Statement on Moral and Spiritual Training in the Schools," 27
Stevenson, William E., 119
Stewart, Justice
   Cramp decision, 141
   Elfbrandt decision, 143
   Engel decision, 27, 29, 47
   Epperson decision, 41, 42
   Flast decision, 40
   Keyishian decision, 146
   Schempp decision, 31, 34, 35
   Shelton decision, 130
   Tinker decision, 134, 135
   Whitehall decision, 145
Story, Justice, 1
Students
   Assignment to desegregated schools, 83, 85, 86, 90, 92
   Assignment to segregated schools, 17, 76, 77, 80
   Attendance at private schools, 82, 88
   Attendance at public schools, 9
   Bus transportation, 9
   Census, 35
   Freedom of speech, 134
   Hair cuts, 133
   Prayer exercises, 27, 37
   Religious instruction, 12, 13
   Textbooks, 8, 38
Supreme Court
   Annual session, 3
   Arguments before the Court, 3
   Attacks on, 4
   Creation of, 1
   Decision day, 3
   Marshal of, 3
   Reversal of decision, 11
   Traditions governing deliberations, 3
   Voting on decisions, 3
Supreme Court building, 2
Supreme Court justices
   Appointment, 1
   Criticisms of, 4
   Number of, 4
   Removal of, 1
   Retirement of, 1
   Seating of, 3
   Term of office, 1
   (*See also* Black, Brandeis, Brennan, Brown, Burton, Byrnes, Chase, Clark, Douglas, Field, Fortas, Frankfurter, Goldberg, Harlan (elder), Harlan (younger), Holmes, Hughes, Jackson, Johnson, Marshal (John), Marshal (Thurgood), McLean, Minton, Murphy, Reed, Roberts, Rutledge, Stewart, Story, Taft, Vinson, Warren, Wayne, White, Whittaker)
Sweatt, Herman, 19

Taft, Justice, 17
Teachers
   Associations, 124, 125, 127, 129, 137
   Desegregation, 93
   Free speech, 132
   Incompetency, 126
   Religious test, 35, 36
   Subversion, 21, 122, 140
   Teaching of evolution, 41
Tennessee, state of, 42
Test, religious, 35, 36
Texas, state of, 18, 75
Textbooks, 8, 38
Time, dismissed, 13
Tinker, John, 134
Tinker, Mary Beth, 134
Transfer plans
   Cahokia, 86
   Knoxville, 85
   Monroe, 92
Transportation
   Douglas' change of position, 60
   Non-public school students, 9
   Railway, 15

Union Free School District, 27
U. S. Reports, 3

Vassar, 127
Vinson, Justice, 2, 18, 19
Virginia, state of, 76-78, 88
Voluntary prayers, 37

Wall of separation, 9, 34, 44
Warren, Justice
   Barenblatt decision, 128

Beilan decision, 127
Bolling decision, 80
Brown ('54) decision, 76, 79, 80, 100, 102, 106, 107
Brown ('55) decision, 81
Cooper decision, 84, 85, 104, 105, 109
Days of announcing decisions, 3
Elfbrandt decision, 143
Flast decision, 40, 41
Keyishian decision, 146
Sweezy decision, 124
Term of service on the Court, 4
Washington, George, 4
Washington, Justice, 1
Washington, state of, 142
Washington, University of, 142
Watkins School, 91
Wayne, Justice, 1

Weigle, Luther A., 58
West Virginia, state of, 11
White, Justice
   Allen decision, 38
   Baggett decision, 142
   Elfbrandt decision, 143, 144
   Engel decision, 28
   Keyishian decision, 146
   Law clerk, 2
   Pickering decision, 132, 133
   Rogers decision, 90
   Tinker decision, 134
   Whitehall decision, 145
Whitehall, Howard Joseph, 144
Whittaker, Justice, 109, 124, 131
Will County, Illinois, 132
Wills, 104
Witnesses, Jehovah's, 10, 11, 25